FINDING *your own* HAPPY

The Soul-Searcher's Guide to Peace and Happiness in Everyday Life

Elana Davidson

NEW YORK

LONDON • NASHVILLE • MELBOURNE • VANCOUVER

Finding Your Own Happy

© 2019 Elana Davidson

Published in New York, New York, by Morgan James Publishing in partnership with Difference Press.
www.MorganJamesPublishing.com

The Morgan James Speakers Group can bring authors to your live event. For more information or to book an event visit The Morgan James Speakers Group at
www.TheMorganJamesSpeakersGroup.com.

ISBN 978-1-64279-034-4 paperback
ISBN 978-1-64279-035-1 eBook
Library of Congress Control Number: 2018938049

Cover & Interior Design by:
Megan Whitney Dillon
Creative Ninja Designs
megan@creativeninjadesigns.com

In an effort to support local communities, raise awareness and funds, Morgan James Publishing donates a percentage of all book sales for the life of each book to Habitat for Humanity Peninsula and Greater Williamsburg.

Get involved today! Visit
www.MorganJamesBuilds.com

For the genuine and authentic expression of self we knew so well in childhood but later somehow lost, and for all those who have the courage to find that place and revive it within themselves.

Contents

Introduction 1

Chapter 1 – Start from Where You Are. 5

Chapter 2 – The Journey to Finding the Keys 9

Chapter 3 – Walking the Path. .19

Chapter 4 – Contexts and Conditions Matter 25

Chapter 5 – A New Way of Seeing 37

Chapter 6 – Awareness is (Almost) Everything 49

Chapter 7 – Know You and Your Own Energy 61

Chapter 8 – Why Therapy Might Not Be Working for You and What
You Can Do About It. 75

Chapter 9 – Move Beyond the Shadows of Your Childhood 87

Chapter 10 – Reset Your Emotional Compass .101

Chapter 11 – Put the Trust Back in You. 113

Chapter 12 – Other Weird Stuff You Need to Know. 125

Chapter 13 – Obstacles on This Path. 137

Conclusion 143

Your Tool Kit for Change. 149

Suggested Further Reading 151

Acknowledgments 153

Thank You 157

About the Author 159

Introduction

"When you come to the edge of all the light you have, and must take a step into the darkness of the unknown, believe that one of two things will happen. Either there will be something solid for you to stand on—or you will be taught how to fly."

PATRICK OVERTON

Do you feel like you've done all the right things, tried all the right tools, processes or therapies, and you're still not all that happy?

You've heard that happiness is a choice, right? But does it feel like a choice for you?

How about, "Change your thinking, change your life."?

Or, "You create your own reality...

You just need to get out more...

To think more positively...

Try a little harder... apply yourself... maybe if you would just...

Cheer up, life isn't that bad. Look at all the great things you have going for you...."

After a while I started to hate all this advice, all these cliché sayings, because my feelings of unhappiness weren't because I wasn't trying. They weren't because I didn't have the right attitude or wasn't thinking the right thoughts. They were so much deeper than that. I'd done so much of that self-help, be-positive, happiness-is-a-choice kind of thing, but despite everything I still didn't feel all that happy. I didn't know why, and I didn't know what to do about it.

No one else did either, because everything they suggested, even if it helped a little, didn't ultimately bring me to a place of being happy. Sure, I could feel a little more happy, but it was like rolling a rock uphill most of the time. As soon as I got the rock up the hill, it would roll right back down.

Exhausting.

Maybe you've tried all those suggestions and they're still not working? Or you're tired of working so hard all the time just to be a little happier? That was totally true for me. I wished I could find someone who could really get it and stop giving me all these surface-level solutions to confusing and complex problems. My unhappiness was not just because I'm not thinking the right thoughts, it was so much more nuanced and complex than that.

I tried the psycho-therapeutic model but it didn't really fit for me and I didn't find it all that helpful. I didn't want to go on drugs and I didn't want to be diagnosed with a mental health disorder. I just wanted to figure out what my real problems were and why I had to work seemingly so much harder than anyone else just to feel happy.

I wished there was someone, some resource, some healer, some psychic, some system or process that could help me understand what was going on with me, and the confusing and challenging emotional and energetic experiences I was having... and not just understand it but give me a solution that could bring me to a new state of being.

I searched and I searched but I came up short, over and over and over again. I got little fragments of information from lots of different places. Once I'd gathered enough information I started to put it together in my own way. Finally, through many years and lots of trial and error I discovered for myself what the missing pieces were.

It was hard and slow-going and sometimes it didn't seem like I was making any progress at all. It still seemed like I was just pushing that boulder up that hill and it still kept rolling down... though maybe the pushing wasn't as hard and the rolling down wasn't as far. Gathering enough information and learning how to use and apply it to myself over time did finally make a lasting and significant difference. Now I know what it means to be happy without trying. Happiness is my natural state of being.

This book is the gathering together of my story and all the insights, tools, and processes that helped me finally find my own happy.

If you've wondered for a long time why happiness seems so much harder for you than it does for everybody else, or why you can't seem to figure it out, this book will offer some of the missing keys and insights that will open the door to creating greater happiness and fulfillment in your life. Each time I offer these keys to others, whether they be friends, clients, or people I encounter in passing, I delight in witnessing the access to greater happiness that it creates.

Happiness may be a choice, but it's only a choice when you have the capacity to choose it. If you don't have all the right information or understanding about what's truly going on for you or what will truly create happiness for you, it can feel like it's an impossible choice to make.

My hope for you in reading this book is that you will see what you've been missing, and instead of feeling pissed off when people tell you to just "think positive," you will understand what truly creates your happiness, and happiness will be a choice that you can easily make.

Chapter One
Start From Where You Are

*"If you always do what you've always done,
you always get what you've always gotten."*

JESSIE POTTER

What's My Problem and Why Can't I Seem to Figure It Out?

How long have you been searching? Searching for an answer to an unknown problem that, if you could solve it, would finally bring you to a place of truly feeling happy and sane in your life?

You might wonder what's wrong with you, why you can't seem to get how to make your life work–to feel happy, normal, sane, like seemingly everyone else. You know something isn't quite right, but you're not really sure what–and if you don't know what your problem is, it's pretty hard to change it. You don't get it either because you're super self-aware, you're an intelligent, caring and conscious human being and it seems like you're doing all the right things.

The things that seem to work so well for others don't seem to work that well for you. Meditation, yoga, affirmations, positive thinking, visualizations, maybe you've done all that, tried all sorts of personal growth and healing work, or even gone to therapy. They may have helped a little but not significantly. You still wonder what your problem is because none of this has changed your life or made it so you're not working incredibly hard just to feel happy.

Have you wished you could have help and guidance and looked for the support and resources? When what you found didn't make the difference, did you feel like you were left to figure it out on your own? How much time and energy did you invest and how many tears did you shed? How alone did you feel? Maybe you wondered if something was uniquely wrong with you that wasn't like anyone else in the world. Perhaps you kept searching for answers and trying different things, and when they still didn't work, your self-esteem plummeted. Each failed attempt made you feel worse about yourself and it started to wear on your self-confidence. *"How come everyone else gets it and I don't?"* you might think.

I imagine that you would like some help that works. Maybe someone who gets you and understands what you're going through without judging? Someone who could guide you and support you, like a wise mentor or a dear friend? Maybe someone who can relate to or has been through the very things you've struggled with: Trying to make sense of this world, not understanding why you still aren't all that happy, weird emotional or energetic experiences you just don't understand, feeling lost, confused, or insane... Someone who doesn't reduce you to some psychological label, but truly seeks to help and understand. You'd love to truly get to the other side of this confusing and crazy experience of life, to be able to consistently feel happy.

What if I told you that were totally possible? How do I know? Because for so many years of my life I struggled and searched for answers to why, after so much work on myself, I still couldn't seem to get and stay happy. Drugs just weren't an option for me; I wanted to get to the source of why I was not happy. I didn't stop searching until I finally found the key information, tools and insights that unlocked me from my suffering and helped me to create true happiness and fulfillment in my life.

In this book I will share with you my story and all the key information, tools, insights, and perspectives that finally turned things around for me. After decades of struggling and searching and at times literally banging my head against the wall, I have discovered some keys that I see are missing for so many of the folks who just can't figure out why they're still not happy. It's not your fault, you couldn't know, because no one is teaching you these things. Until now. I had to figure all of this out on my own, and it took me a very long time. Figuring out how to put all of the pieces together in the right ways finally made a real and lasting difference for me. Now, I no longer feel depressed or crazy, I've put my life together in a way that works for me, and for the most part, I feel happy. Continue with me on this journey while I share with you my story and the particular key tools, insights and perspectives that finally made a lasting difference. They could be the keys to greater happiness and fulfillment in life that you have also been missing.

Chapter Two
The Journey to Finding the Keys

"...A joy, a depression, a meanness,
Some momentary awareness comes
As an unexpected visitor.
Welcome and entertain them all,
Even if they are a crowd of sorrows
Who violently sweep your house
Of all it's furniture.
Still treat each guest honorably.
She may be cleaning you out for some new delight..."

RUMI

Pondering the Meaning of Life

don't know when it started, but it started when I was quite young. By the time I was twelve I was seriously questioning the point of life and what I was doing here. I was not entirely sure if I wanted to be here at all, and sometimes I felt pretty sure I didn't want to be. In a great big world that I didn't get and that didn't seem to get me, and with no one to truly guide me, I felt incredibly lost, confused and alone.

The teen years intensified my experiences to the point where I was literally banging my head against the wall. I would think about jumping out my second story dorm room window at the boarding school I attended, because I couldn't take my internal pain. I would even bite the back of my hand in response to my inner anguish and frustration. I recognize now that I was screaming for someone to notice me, to pay attention, to care about me and the pain I was in, but it just frightened them and never brought the love, attention, care, support, or guidance that I was crying out for but didn't know how to effectively request.

I'm not going to tell you my whole life story, but what I will tell you is that for so many years it felt like I struggled more than I thrived. My life was often shadowed by emotional turmoil and episodes of depression– though depression is not a word I would have used to describe my experiences at that time. I just thought I was a deep person, going through lots of soul-searching and through perpetual challenge and upheaval in my life. I wondered what was wrong with me that I felt so many twisted up feelings and had so many internal struggles. I thought that I just needed to work on myself and my issues and gain greater spiritual insight and understanding.

I seemed to have so many perpetual challenges with my life, and I didn't believe that anyone else would be able to help me or truly understand. Mostly people proved me right and didn't. I could not point to some horrible thing that had happened to me to make my life so full of pain or feel like such a struggle. In light of that my suffering seemed especially unjustified and wrong. I seemed to have no right or reason to feel so unhappy–a point of view that was re-enforced in various ways both by my family as well as many other people in my life. This confirmed to me that it must just be me that was the problem and that I was in some way flawed, defective, or broken. I thought that if I could just fix what was wrong with me, my life could work and I could finally be happy.

Though my life seemed to have a lot more turmoil and emotionality to it than a lot of other people's, and it wasn't uncommon that I'd experience suicidal feelings of depression, I still hadn't fully acknowledged that I had a problem. I didn't want to be labeled; I didn't want to be seen as defective or wrong even though, ironically, I was seeing myself that way. I just wanted to be seen, and heard, and loved, and helped to heal my pain.

Searching for a Way to Peace and Happiness in Life

I was just trying to make life work for me and trying to be happy and have both things at the same time. So often it seemed that I was choosing between happiness and work, between happiness and where I was living, between happiness and family or friends. Sometimes I truly was happy, but often I was not. I was searching to make sense of this life and for personal understanding of my experience of the human condition. I read lots of spiritual and self-help books from authors like Louise Hay, Eckhart Tolle, and Carolyn Myss, to name a few. I attended spiritual and personal development retreats and studied Non-Violent Communication. I went on vision quests. I spent ten days at a stretch in rigorous silent meditation courses where I could not talk, read, or write and was essentially alone with my own mind. I studied *A Course in Miracles*, working through the entire workbook twice. I explored and applied the work of Byron Katie. I did EFT (emotional freedom technique).

By my late twenties I had even been to therapy, along with seeing so very many other alternative practitioners and healers. Everything helped a little. It gave me insight into myself and my experiences, and provided greater personal understanding. It all helped me navigate my challenging experiences and get better at coping with them, but it didn't change the nature or frequency of those experiences, or reduce my sense of hardship and challenge with life. I'd seem to be going along okay, or even doing well, and then things would just fall apart or get hard and feel crazy again. Despite all of my self-awareness and spiritual knowledge, life was still hard, sad, and lonely more than it was fun, happy, or easy, and it seemed to be a lot harder, sadder, and lonelier than it was for those around me.

Acknowledging That I Have a Problem

In my early thirties, I took a job working with pregnant and parenting teens. Part of my job was to screen these teen parents for signs and symptoms of depression. That's when it finally dawned on me that I might be depressed, and when I finally admitted that I had a problem. I looked back over my adult life and realized that it was not normal to have the frequency of struggle and unhappiness thatI had had. Most other people my same age were not going through the crisis after crisis and struggle after struggle that I seemed to be encountering (though of course, there were also some that were). I saw single teen moms with much harder life conditions than I had who seemed to feel positive, upbeat and happy about their lives. I knew something wasn't right when they seemed so much happier than I was, and *I* was the one supposed to be helping *them*.

I'd like to say that this realization made the difference for me and I found the help I needed and turned my life around. Unfortunately, it didn't quite work that way. I wish I could tell you that there was one magical turning point where I got the answer to my problems and they all just disappeared and went away. It wasn't like I just went to therapy and that fixed everything, or I discovered this one special practice or technique that made all the difference. That, in part, is what sometimes felt so frustrating. I kept looking for that one thing, that one change to my life, that one guide or mentor, that one perfect opportunity that was going to make all the difference for me and magically change everything.

Finding the Keys

What I didn't realize until later was that each new insight or understanding was a piece of the puzzle, and that in order to have true success on this journey, I needed all the pieces and I needed to be able to fit them all together in the right way. Unfortunately, there was no one else who had all the pieces or could show me how they went together to finally transform my experience and bring me to the place of truly being happy. It took me another several years to fully identify the missing pieces and fit them all together in a way that truly made the difference I'd been seeking.

A lot of what this book is about is what I discovered on that journey, how those pieces helped me transform my experience of life, and how they can help you do the same. Fast forward to today: My life looks vastly different than it did even just a couple of years ago. I have a home and job I truly like, and I haven't felt suicidal or truly depressed in years. Life certainly isn't perfect and there's always room for improvement, but I know how to access my own happiness, and when I lose it, I know exactly what I need to do to get it back.

Even in the process of writing this book I've come to moments of feeling unhappy or dissatisfied with some aspect of my life. I start to wonder if I have a right to be writing this book to help people shift their experiences when it seems that I'm still struggling with mine. Then I ask myself if I've applied the tools and insights contained within these pages, and the answer is almost always no. As soon as I put what I'm teaching to use, my feelings shift and my experience changes and I come back to feeling happy again. It hasn't been just sometimes, it's been every single time. I have the necessary tools and information for accessing my own happiness and they work–but only if I use them.

What I Mean By Happy

Let me define what I mean by "happy." I'm not implying that having a smile on your face and being super upbeat and enthusiastic about life all the time is the optimal state of being. The feeling of happiness, like any other emotion, is a feeling which rightly comes and goes. At certain times the most appropriate emotion to be feeling is not happiness. If you get hard news, or are facing a challenge, then the emotion of happiness might not be the most likely or even appropriate emotional response. What I'm talking about in this book when I'm talking about being happy is a general sense of well-being and contentment or peace with life. I can be sad, I can have tears streaming down my face, and still be in that place of happiness, in a place where I can be connected to my okayness and my okayness with life. In a sense it's the absence of deep inner conflict, anguish, turmoil, and confusion–that is the happiness of which I speak. The opposite of happy in this sense is not the experience of sadness, but more the deadness, numbness, or anguish and lack of vitality or energy for life. Happiness is a sense of harmony with one's self even when facing the inevitable challenges of life.

How I Came to Help Others

Somewhere along this journey I realized that because of the depth of my own challenge and struggle, and because of my temperament, I had the capacity to sit with other people's pain. It doesn't scare me. Your suicidal feelings don't scare me. I've been there, maybe worse than there. I know what it's like to suffer emotionally. I also know what it's like to be judged, or have someone try to fix me or change me in ways that don't feel genuine or helpful or when I'm not yet ready.

I knew what I needed that I wasn't getting, and I discovered that at times I could be that person for other people. As I progressed along my journey and found more and more keys to my own happiness, I began to share them with others and help them access theirs. I have always had a calling to help other people, I just wasn't sure what form it would take.

For years I worked with children, relating deeply to their experiences and their challenges and wishing to provide them with true love, support, and guidance—things that felt essential to their well-being—and that I felt were often missing in my own life. In a way, my work with children has led me to the work I do now. So much of the work of coaching and healing is in one way or another about healing or transforming our childhood pain. (My work with children was so much about how to engage with them in ways that would not inflict that pain in the first place.) As life calls me to step more and more into the role of coach, mentor, and healer, I'm helping others navigate the territory and path that I struggled with for so long, making their travel time shorter and their journey easier. I'm helping them find their way out of their struggles and inner turmoil and to true peace and happiness in their lives.

Imagine a Different Possibility for Yourself

Imagine that you could wake up every day feeling happy. You're looking forward to your day, to the things you get to do, the life you have and the future you're creating. Your life is permeated by a general sense of happiness and overall well-being. Sure, there are still things you're working toward or that could be different, but for the most part you feel happy and good in yourself and with your life. Even on the days that are a little bumpy, you know what to do or change to get back to a place of feeling good and happy again. You are no longer mystified by your experiences or stuck with moods or emotional experiences you don't know how to change.

From this place, it feels so much easier to connect with other people, to pursue the things you're interested in, and even have fun. People smile at you or want to be around you because they enjoy your presence and your energy. They compliment and appreciate you for the contributions and value you bring to their lives. You like and feel good about yourself, and you truly enjoy who you are. You carry yourself with confidence. You have a sense of expectancy, hope, and possibility for your life.

Maybe you're thinking, *"that is totally not me."* Maybe this isn't you, but could it be? Could you entertain it as a possibility? In my worst and even my moderately okay moments, I didn't really consider that that could be my reality. I just wanted to feel okay, to be able to function normally and to get through my day and my life in a moderately okay feeling way. The peace, ease, happiness, and self-confidence that have emerged for me are so different and yet so much greater than I ever could have imagined.

It certainly wasn't easy to get here. And it took me a *reaaaally looooooooong* time, like twenty plus years of searching, but I can finally say that I am happy in myself and with life. Now that I've found this place, I can also see that if I'd known and understood some key things about myself and my experiences, I could have been living a truly happy and fulfilling life so much sooner.

There Is Another Way

What if you knew what you truly needed to do to get to greater happiness and what if you had the necessary guidance about how to go about doing it? You picked up this book for a reason. Does it have something to offer you? Are you willing to read it? More than that, not just read it, but also put into practice what is being offered here? It's easy to stand on the outside and intellectually judge or attempt to evaluate the merits of something, but you must also practice it, do it, and live it to know what truth or value it really holds. If you only *read* this book, you will gain something–perhaps some insight or intellectual understanding–but if you put what I am sharing into practice in your own life, you will relate to it and understand it in an entirely different way. The keys to the kingdom of happiness only work if you put them in the lock and turn them. What I offer you in this book are some of the missing keys that will help you create greater happiness and fulfillment in your life.

Chapter Three
Walking the Path

*"Be patient toward all that is unsolved in your heart
and try to love the questions themselves."*

RAINER MARIA RILKE

After decades of searching and feeling lost as I looked for my own happiness, I do believe that I have found the necessary keys that give me and my clients access to greater happiness and fulfillment in our lives. As I go along my own journey and inevitably hit bumps or challenges along the way, I have yet to find something in my life experience that has not been shifted or fundamentally changed by using one (or more) of these perspectives, tools, and processes.

Let me take you on a little tour of where we're headed. I'll show you the path I've set out for us before we begin the journey together.

The Context in Which Your Problem Exists

We'll take a look at the contexts and the conditions around you and how they might influence you or affect your experiences and behavior. When you understand the context in which your problem or challenge exists, it can give you a different perspective and help influence and support how you work with it. Some of your struggle is in direct relationship to this context, and when you change the context, some of your "problems" may just go away. The context is like the water in which you swim. Swimming in a choppy ocean is going to be very different than a smooth, calm lake, though you and your swimming abilities are the same.

A New Framework for Working with Your Experiences

You'll understand a different way of approaching your experiences and challenges that can lead you to very different outcomes than what you've accomplished before. This framework will guide and inform the rest of the work in this book.

If the context in which your problem exists is like the water in which you swim, then this new framework is how to do the swimming. It will look very different from how you learned to swim before.

Imagine that you were only ever taught to swim with your face in the water. When you swim face down, you're always looking at the bottom. You have to learn how to breathe so you don't run out of air, you have to work very hard to keep yourself up. You swallow water and can't seem to get the breathing right. It's hard and slow-going and often frustrating. It never even occurred to you that there could be another way of swimming. The idea that you could swim on your back just never entered your awareness. Swimming on your back is so much easier and such a different view. You can stay up with practically no effort, breathing comes easily, and whatever little efforts you do make seem to yield much greater results than they ever did before. You wonder why, in all your life, it never occurred to you to swim on your back. Now that you know this, everything is different, and you have a whole new approach to work with. This section will be like learning new ways of swimming.

Identify What's Actually Yours

Next, I'll help you get clear on what is truly yours to fix. At times it can be easy to take on other people's issues and problems and for them to start to bog you down. Progress is pretty slow-going when you're carrying everybody else on your back! We'll look at one of the main obstacles that has kept you struggling and suffering for a needlessly long time, and what you can do to change it. I'll give you practical tools that will help you easily let go of anyone else you are carrying (unless of course you want to carry them!) and be able to make positive forward progress for yourself.

Reclaim Your Energy from Everyone Else

Next, I will give you practical tools and techniques for working with and managing your energy and helping you stay in a feeling-good place throughout your day and your life. These are tools and techniques that have made a significant difference in my emotional experiences of life. You'll see where and how your energy and vitality have been getting diminished or drained and what you can do to recover them again.

Why Therapy Hasn't Worked for You and What to Do Instead

If therapy has worked or is working for you, great, don't change that! However, if you're reading this book, I'm guessing that you've either gone to therapy and it hasn't worked for you–at least not well enough–or the whole model of therapy just seems off to you and you haven't bothered trying it. I'll share some of the key reasons why that might have been the case, including what most approaches, even alternative therapies and other healing modalities, are missing. You'll more clearly understand why therapy hasn't worked for you and how to move in a direction that is more effective and empowering than what you've experienced in the past. I'll give you the main keys that therapy is often missing, and show you how to use them to unlock new insights, shifts, and healing for your self.

Moving Beyond the Shadow of Your Childhood Experiences

So much of our internal and emotional challenges have their roots in our childhood experience. I'll give you some new insight and understanding to the dynamics present in childhood and how they may be continuing to affect you (with or without you knowing it) throughout your adult life. I'll also give you tools to help you transform and move beyond them so that they no longer hold you back or feel like major obstacles or challenges.

Resetting Your Emotional Compass

Chances are you had to learn some pretty creative coping mechanisms to survive the experiences of your life. You probably, like virtually all of us, learned ways to manage and control your emotional responses to things. This may have helped you get through life and survive but it didn't necessarily contribute to your happiness. We'll untangle and reset the places where your emotional experiences have become confused or tangled up so that they can be helpful guides for you. They'll be able to provide you with truly valuable information that can empower you and help you better navigate your life.

Keys to Trusting Yourself and Your Awareness

How much do you doubt or question yourself, your choices, your experiences of things, or your very reality? If you're like so very many of my clients, you're questioning and doubting yourself a lot! I used to doubt and question myself a lot too, even to the brink of driving myself crazy. I was finally able to shift that, and will be sharing with you some keys to cultivating a greater degree of trust in yourself and your awareness. Trust is like a muscle: The more you trust you, the more you *can* trust you. These keys will teach you how to begin developing that muscle and build a greater sense of confidence and trust in yourself.

Other Weird Stuff You Need to Know

I put the above content together intending to include all the necessary tools and information that have helped me shift any experience or internal challenge in my life. I realized, however, that there are a few additional necessary tools and some important information that have been left out in the preceding chapters. I needed to include them in order for this information to truly be complete. They don't fit neatly into any particular category, but they have, nevertheless, at times been what was required to change my experiences when nothing else seemed to work: entities, bodies, chakras, and projections. I give them to you in this chapter so that you have everything I have used to find my way to happy and unlock myself from any challenging feelings or states of being that I experience.

Challenges on the Path

Every journey has its obstacles, its pitfalls, its likely challenges and wrong turns, places where you might think you're lost and stuck or have failed with the process. That is an inevitable part of the journey. However, if I tell you what to watch out for, and where you might get tripped up, lost, or stuck, and how to either get out of those places or avoid them all together, you will be able to travel with much more ease and to more quickly find your way to happy. You will have an easier time getting back on track when you've gotten off track and can continue to create a life for yourself that is filled with the kind of happiness and peace you've been searching for and not finding for so many years of your life.

This is just the beginning. If you take the time and work through these key areas, you will have a solid foundation on which to build. I have seen repeatedly how trying to build or create your life without taking care of these foundational elements first just leaves your creations on shaky ground at best, and often ends with them tumbling down around you. Let's create that solid foundation together so that you can keep moving toward successfully creating the life you truly desire.

Chapter Four
Contexts and Conditions Matter

*"Before you diagnose yourself with depression
or low self-esteem, first make sure that you
are not, in fact, just surrounded by a**holes."*

NOTORIOUS D.E.B.

W hat if I told you that so many of your feelings and experiences are completely justified and normal and that your struggles might have more to do with the context and conditions you are in than something that is inherently wrong with you?. How much do you blame yourself and think it is you and your own personal shortcomings that keep you from a happy and fulfilling life? That you are the problem, and that if you could just change you, then everything could be fine? What if the contexts and conditions you are in have a greater impact on you than you have ever been willing to consider?

Emotionally Appropriate Responses
to the Context You Are in

It is very easy in our Western society and culture to blame the individual. Often, our approach to mental health goes something like this: Figure out what's wrong with the person, give them a diagnosis, put them on medications, and that should solve their problem. If it doesn't, change the dose or prescriptions until it does. Even with more therapeutic-based approaches, by and large the focus is only on the individual's personal or family problems and does not look at the larger context in which those problems exist.

What if this is missing a very important piece? What if, in some cases, what a person is experiencing is in direct relationship to the context they are in? What if they are having an emotionally appropriate response to the conditions and environments of their life? A few years ago I read a statistic that particularly shocked me: "The fastest growing population on anti-depressants is kindergartners." *Kindergartners!!* What? I've worked with children much of my life and I find this particularly alarming. Given our current education system, which is often at odds with children's true developmental needs, their depression may very well be an emotionally appropriate response. I guarantee you that if you changed the environment of those children to one that was truly developmentally appropriate, supportive, and nurturing, most of these same children would not display the signs and symptoms that lead them to be prescribed anti-depressant medications. That, however, is much harder than deciding the problem is just with individual children. It is easier to pathologize the individual and treat their symptoms than to change the whole system or to examine the context and conditions they are in. What if part of what is going on for you is that you are having emotionally appropriate responses to the environments and conditions of your life?

Have you ever heard of the canary in the coal mine? Canaries are affected by toxic gases in the mines much sooner than the miners. They are indicators of dangers yet to come. They are the sensitive ones. They know there is a problem before others are even aware that there is any danger. I have often thought that those of us who have had a difficult time adjusting to life on planet earth and the disconnected world that most of us live in are a bit like those canaries—we sense and perceive long before others do that there is something missing, something out of balance that is not supporting our well-being and our thriving, not just individually but also collectively. *To be sane in an insane world is to be insane.*

What Is the Actual Problem?

You might be wondering, *"What does this have to do with me and my problems and figuring out how to be happy?"* Well, what conditions or circumstances are you in? Are they truly supportive to you and your well-being? Who are the people around you? Do they truly see you, value you, support you? How do you feel when you're with them?

I spent a lot of time thinking that I was the problem, and if I could just fix me, then everything would be fine. Except I could never get to the source of what my problem was. I'd look at myself, work on myself some more, do better, be better, nicer, kinder, and yet *why am I still so unhappy, why do I feel so miserable, why can't I get my life to work*? I still couldn't find the problems I could fix that would create the changes I desired. I also wasn't allowing myself to see or feel the impact of what was happening around me or to have an emotionally appropriate response to the context and conditions I was in.

My family conveniently perceived me as the problem too, because then they didn't have to look at themselves or their behavior or take stock of what I was seeing. The truth is, I was aware of dynamics and dysfunctions within my family that my parents weren't willing to acknowledge or see. They just turned them back onto me as a problem with me. Because they weren't willing to validate or acknowledge the truth of what I was seeing, I also cut myself off from it and made me wrong instead. Pathologize the individual, don't consider the context or the system. I was the one that was the problem and there was no room to acknowledge that there may have been something else going on to which I was having an emotionally appropriate response, like my parents' lack of emotional support or availability.

I think my parents were well intended, but I would say that they were quite oblivious to some pretty important things. When I tried to point them out, they just told me I was wrong and that it was just me that had the problem. Once I started to unravel this and to see that there was some validity to my perceptions and experiences that other people outside my immediate family could see and acknowledge even if my parents couldn't, I stopped feeling so weird, screwed up and insane. I could now see that maybe I was having an appropriate response to dynamics within my family. Once I got this, I stopped trying to get my parents to see how they weren't showing up for me or not treating me all that kindly, and just acknowledged what was true for me. I was then able to embark on the journey toward creating a life that worked for me and in which I was truly happy.

What if you're not actually broken, screwed up and in need of fixing? What if you're incredibly sensitive, incredibly aware? What if you perceive things that other people aren't willing to perceive or acknowledge? Not because they are bad people, but because they don't have the same perceptive abilities as you do? Does that ring true for you? Perhaps for others to perceive and acknowledge what you see would require such a departure from how they have constructed their understanding of the world that it would be more of a disruption to their sense of reality than they are willing to endure. I now get why my mom needed to hold on to the narrative that she was nothing but a wonderful and supportive mother and that I was the one with all the problems. It would have destroyed her sense of herself and her reality to see otherwise. Because I was able to validate my experience for myself and know that my experiences and perceptions were not crazy, I no longer needed her to get it and could just let her be. That was the beginning of freedom: trusting my perceptions and validating myself and my own reality, and knowing that maybe I wasn't always the one that was screwed up and crazy!

Spiritual Awakening: What It Really Looks Like Vs. What We Think It Looks Like

We can be tempted to think that if we are getting it right, if we are on the correct path to personal development and to spiritual awakening then our lives should be joyful, bliss-filled, and easy. If anything other than that is showing up, we may think that we have gotten something wrong. Ironically, life does get more joyful and easy, blissful even, but when we're in the process of awakening or spiritual transformation, it can feel quite the opposite. You might be tempted to judge and blame yourself, or to think that because things feel intense or hard that you are failing. Could it be, however, that whatever intensity is showing up, whatever energy or challenge you are experiencing, is exactly what you need to face and rise above to move to a greater place of ease, joy, and happiness in your life?

I know it can feel horrible, but if you stop there and don't see your way through, don't recognize that this may be part of your spiritual initiation, you will miss a great opportunity for learning and growing and for experiencing the happiness that you are seeking. Sometimes we are spinning around in circles, not getting what we need to learn or looking in the wrong places for the answers, and sometimes the hard places are invitations to become more, to step more fully into our power.

When I was in college I took a class on Shamanisms. One thing that stuck with me from that class is these various different cultures' completely different relationships to suffering and spiritual awakening. Shamans would struggle with some horrendous condition, issue, or challenge—sometimes for decades of their lives—as part of their initiation into being a shaman. Many of their rituals and rites of passage include enduring and triumphing over extreme physical challenge, pain or highly adverse conditions, and according to their traditions, there is a supreme value and spiritual benefit in this. It is part of how you evolve spiritually. I don't 100% buy the "no pain, no gain" adage, but I think there is some truth in it. Pain and suffering are invitations, are motivations for transformation, for transcending or triumphing over your experience and developing greater inner capacities as a result. As we learn to listen to ourselves and more quickly adjust our path, then we don't require such intense or painful experiences to get our attention and wake us up.

When I found myself going through some extreme intensity or challenge, or it seemed to be repeating, or going on for what seemed a long time (maybe months compared to decades for those shamans I read about in college), I would re-frame my understanding of personal transformation from the sanitized version I received from my new-age upbringing to this more shamanic one. Birth and growth are often messy, challenging, and painful, yet, when we rise to the occasion and find the way through them, we come out the other side with such greater wisdom, understanding and capacities. What if you see the challenges and intensities that show up in your life as part of your spiritual initiation? How would you approach them or show up differently to them then? How do you rise, face, and triumph over the challenge?

When you're in the middle of something intense, it can be tempting to judge it and create a story around the wrongness of it. But what if this is truly part of your initiation and is required to bring you to a new place in your life? Ultimately, what choice do you have? You can stay where you are and continue to suffer, you can judge, blame, avoid, or resist, or you can choose to face the challenge, rise to the occasion, and find your way to something greater. The choice is truly yours. If you're ready to rise to the occasion, then I'm here to help guide you through the process. I can accompany you on your journey, help you to understand it, and share with you the information, tools, and guidance that will empower and help you to step into a greater place in yourself and your life. It will ultimately bring you to that greater ease, joy, and happiness you've been seeking.

Stop Tolerating Unfavorable Conditions

If you're ready, let's begin.

Let's begin by looking at some of the conditions and contexts in your life that are less than supportive to your well-being. What are you tolerating but you aren't actually happy with? Tolerance is something that people often tout as a virtue, but it can often mean not fully choosing what you would like and putting up with conditions, people and circumstances that don't support you or your well-being. Context and conditions do matter!

Why do we tolerate things that make us feel like crap about ourselves and our lives and that are slowly draining the life from our beings? Mostly we tolerate out of fear. Fear that if we stop tolerating, we won't get anything better. We'll have nothing instead of what little we do have: fear, doubt, or lack of trust that we *can* have what we truly desire and must settle for something less. We tolerate because we fear the consequences of expressing our true desires, of saying and going for what we truly want. We don't want to hurt, bother, or offend others. We are afraid of what others will think of our choices. We may believe that *if we just work on our issues a little more, just shift something in our consciousness, perspective, giving, or being then things will finally change for better.* Yet, sometimes making different choices or choosing different circumstances is our most powerful tool for creating positive change in our lives.

Have you bought the idea that you should stick with things and not give up when it gets hard? That you should never quit? Sometimes that can be a real virtue. Working through the hard stuff can bring beautiful gifts and rewards. However, in my experience both personally and with clients, more often than not, we've tried for way too long to make things work, hold them together, work them out, or otherwise manage situations that didn't support us or work for us in the long run. Most of the time some part of us knew it wasn't what we wanted, even if we weren't willing to admit it to ourselves at the time. When we try so hard to make things work, we are usually just prolonging our discomfort and unhappiness, and have not been willing to listen to our truth about the situation. Often, it is this very effort that has kept us in the less than enjoyable, supportive, or positive environments and conditions we are in.

How many times have you stuck with something or someone and tried to make it work when it really just didn't? How much suffering could you have saved yourself and others if you were very clear about what did and didn't work for you or what you did or didn't want? What would your life be like if you were a little less willing to endure circumstances and conditions that don't support you or your well-being? I know you think that you *have to* stay, that there isn't another option and you have to stick with the reality and conditions you are in. Is that really true? How much is that point of view keeping you in unfavorable conditions?

I was in a situation where I both lived and worked in an environment that was becoming extremely unhealthy and un-supportive to my well-being. I kept trying to make it work, I kept stretching. It was in a rural town where I knew hardly anyone and I had no idea what I would do or where I would go if I left. I was scared of being jobless, homeless, and virtually alone, so I kept on staying–until I could not tolerate even another day. Without knowing what would come, where I would go or what I would do, I let the woman I was living with know that I was done and would be moving on. That very day, someone else put me in touch with folks who were trying to sell their house who wanted someone to live in it for free until it sold. I also found a job right down the street from that house. Sometimes the answer comes after you make the choice or decision to make the change.

Let's have a look at some of the unfavorable contexts and conditions in which you currently experience life. Then, let's look at what we can change to create something that works better for you and creating the life that you desire.

Change the Contexts to Ones That Are Life-Supporting

1. **Make a list of all the things in your life that you're tolerating or putting up with that don't contribute to your thriving.** Anything and everything that doesn't feel like it contributes to you and your well-being can go onto this list. Whatever it is just write it down. It could be relationships you have, how much sleep you get, the kind of work you're doing, how you're eating or taking care of your body, or the place where you're living, anything you're less than happy with and wish would change.

2. **How many can you eliminate from your life right now?** Then choose to do so, and cross them off your list!

3. **Of the ones you don't think you can eliminate from your life right now, ask yourself these questions:**

   - Why am I continuing to choose this or have this in my life?

   - What does it cost me to continue tolerating this?

   - What will my life look like in one, three, or five years if I don't shift or change this?

   - What would I need to change or do in order for this to be different?

   - What choices can I make that would help to change this?

4. **Cross off whatever new ones you're able to cross off, either because you realize that you actually want them in your life, or because you can easily choose to let them go or create something different.** You might realize you're choosing to

have that annoying uncle in your life because there's some other value in the relationship you don't want to give up, or that a job that you don't love is supporting you in getting somewhere else you want to go, so you're willing to stick with it for now. When you recognize that you're *choosing* it instead of just putting up with it, then that inner tension and conflict about not doing what you want to do or being unhappy with where you are can start to subside–either that or you can work on creating something different, but either way you stop being as much of a victim of your circumstances and your life.

5. **For what is still on this list, choose three that you will take action to change.** You could start with what you think would be the easiest, or the ones that feel the most critical or important. What choices can you make or steps can you take to change them? Is there something you need to learn? Is there someone you could talk to? What would it take to truly change them? When those have changed, cross them off your list and choose three more. Keep doing this until you have crossed out everything.

The goal is to no longer have a list–either because you shift your perspective, see the value and accept what you were once "tolerating," or make a new choice toward something that is in greater alignment with your being. Then you have either chosen or made peace with the context and conditions in which you live, or you have empowered yourself to make the necessary changes in your life. You don't have to just passively accept the unpleasant contexts and conditions you are in. It might not always be easy to change what's not working for you, but the first step is to acknowledge what isn't working and to choose to do whatever is in your power to change it. That, or accept and make peace with where you are.

Chapter Five
A New Way of Seeing

"You do not have to be good.
You do not have to walk on your knees
For a hundred miles through the desert, repenting.
You only have to let the soft animal
of your body love what it loves..."

MARY OLIVER

End the War with Yourself

Have you ever noticed how often you make yourself wrong? Fight yourself, argue with your experience, think that you should be different? Judge yourself for feeling what you're feeling? Maybe you tell yourself, *"Why am I feeling this way? I shouldn't feel this way."* If you're feeling something undesirable or unpleasant, do you wonder what is wrong with you and why it won't just go away? Do you go about trying to change it, trying to change yourself?

I did this on pretty much a daily basis. One morning, about to go into the usual sparring match with myself, I had a total shift of perspective. I wondered if maybe what I was experiencing might serve some purpose. What if my feelings weren't just something negative that I needed to change or get rid of? What if they weren't a personality or character defect, something broken about me that I needed to fix? What if they might have a valuable purpose that is part of my design? Think of nature: Everything in nature has some sort of function, design, or purpose; it's not just defective and broken. I started to question this whole notion that unpleasant emotional experience means that we as human beings are somehow broken or flawed. I started to wonder if maybe we work exceptionally well, but we just don't properly understand how we work, and have been misinterpreting our experiences as something defective rather than a valuable part of our design.

That's when I stopped making myself wrong for all the unpleasant feelings I was having. Instead, I started to inquire into them from the point of view that there was some purpose or wisdom to them, and if I could learn to understand them, they could have important information for me.

The True Purpose of Your Feelings

One of the things my study and practice of Nonviolent Communication has taught me is that our feelings arise in direct relationship to our basic human needs–those core needs we all share as human beings–things like shelter and water, but also things like consideration, understanding, and respect. Our feelings are indicators of those needs. When we're hungry it indicates a need for nourishment, when we're thirsty it indicates a need for hydration, when we're tired, we have a need for rest or sleep.

We might push ourselves or not attend to the needs these experiences are indicating, but for the most part we don't argue with them. If you're thirsty, it is unlikely that you would think, *"What the hell is wrong with me, why am I feeling thirsty? I need to figure out how to stop feeling thirsty."* Yet, is that not what you do with some of your other feelings? What if every feeling you have is also connected to a need? What if your feelings are just signals, alerting you to pay attention to those basic human needs? What if they are part of the intelligence of your design?

The morning that I had this change of perspective, I began the usual mental gymnastics of trying to figure out how to change the way I was feeling because I didn't like it very much. Then I stopped myself. I began to connect with my feelings and inquire into my experience with this new perspective in mind. When I stopped the inner heckling and debate about how to change my feelings and paid attention to them, they held valuable information for me. When I was willing to truly listen, the unpleasant feelings actually went away.

"What is this feeling, and what might it be telling me?" I asked myself. If feelings are truly just indicators of my needs, then what needs do I have right now that are not being met? In this instance what my listening revealed was that I was not at all happy with my living situation–there were many needs going unmet, and my feelings were indicating to me that something needed to change. When I acknowledged that and made the decision to make some necessary changes, things shifted, and I felt at peace with myself again. I then made those changes and my experience of life quickly improved.

A second, and equally important, understanding of Nonviolent Communication is that all human behavior is driven out of a desire to meet needs, and that all anyone is ever doing is trying to meet their needs.

Even our seemingly self-destructive behavior is often an attempt to meet needs in some way. When we can identify that and get to what's behind our actions, we have much greater power to change our behavior to something more self-supporting.

Everything is Information You Can Use to Your Advantage

Through my work with clients using the process of Transformational Kinesiology (more about that later) and through my own experiences, I have come to the perspective that everything that is going on for us has a life-serving purpose or function, whether we are aware of it or not. All of our experiences contain useful information about ourselves that can be used to our advantage. Whether it's understanding the needs that my feelings are pointing to, or uncovering subconscious beliefs that are contributing to my experiences and behaviors, once I reach a level of true understanding of what is behind my experience or behavior, it changes.

What I see over and over again is that, when we get the full picture and understand what is truly going on, our experiences, our choices, and our behavior make perfect sense. I'm not talking necessarily about the external conditions of your life or the circumstances you find yourself in, though there's interesting information there as well. I'm talking about your habits and behaviors as well as your inner and emotional experiences, the places you feel less than wonderful, stuck, frustrated, broken, screwed up or wrong. Even debilitating or suicidal depression has an underlying message, something that is behind it, a root cause. Every time I can trace my experiences back to that source, back to the root of what is going on inside me, I come back to a place of ease, peace, and hope with life. I have literally been curled up in a ball, feeling like I couldn't move, and have been able to shift that place by inquiring into it and understanding how it is serving me, what it's telling me, or what is underneath it. After years of struggle with depression and not understanding what was going on for me or how to change it, I now understand the dynamics that contribute to these types of experiences and feelings. On the now relatively rare occasions that feelings of depression occur in my life, I have the keys to understanding that fully liberates me from them (which is, of course, a lot of what I'll be sharing with you in this book).

What's Behind Your Experiences: Stay Curious and Ask Questions

How do you begin to identify what's behind your experiences and find the information that can set you free? One of the ways to do this is to move out of judgment and conclusion and stay in question and curiosity about everything. Questions allow for new input and information, whereas judgments and conclusions limit you to what you've already decided and concluded is true.

How many times have you gotten some difficult news or been faced with a challenging situation and gone into a whole bunch of judgments and conclusions about what it means? Let's say you just lost your job. Chances are you'll immediately make a bunch of conclusions about what that means. *"I'm not going to have any money, I won't be able to pay my rent, I'm going to be homeless and on the streets."* Sound at least a little bit familiar? From there, how much room do you have to perceive a different possibility? How much are you now convinced that this is the truth of your situation, and nothing else is even a possibility? How great does that feel?

Now let's see what happens when we question instead, *"I wonder what else I can do now? I wonder what other possibilities are available to me now that weren't before? What would I truly like to do, who could I talk to?"* *"how could this turn out better than I could have imagined or planned?"* *"what's great about this that I haven't been willing to see or imagine?"* You get the idea. Does staying in the question feel very different from all those conclusions you had? Most people who get fired from or lose their jobs, were either unhappy there or wanted to leave anyway, but just did not have the courage to do it. Could it actually be that this is the universe giving you what you've been asking for and facilitating something greater for you? Could that also be true in lots of other situations?

This staying out of judgments and conclusions and in curiosity and question also applies on the emotional level. Let's say you're not feeling very happy. What if you didn't judge it and instead started asking questions? *"Is this even my unhappiness or is this just something that I'm aware of? What needs could this unhappiness be pointing to for me? What am I aware of here and what is life trying to communicate to me?"* Notice what feels light to you. Can you see that those questions all point to a different possibility than just confirming how unhappy you are? What's true for you will make you feel lighter. My compass and gauge is if something feels lighter, easier, or makes my life feel better, then I'm moving in the right direction and there's some truth for me in it.

One key to unlocking myself from depression was to stop judging myself for it. Some mornings I didn't want to get out of bed. I judged myself and had lots of conclusions about the wrongness of it. Then I said, *"Okay, so what if I don't want to get out of bed? It doesn't have to mean all the things I've decided that it means."* I was amazed at how much my experience shifted when I stopped judging it and demanding that it change. In the space of allowance and acceptance, something different was able to show up in my life–the judgment and wrongness were what kept me stuck where I was. No, I didn't stay in bed for the rest of my life, or even all day every day as I may have feared. I just gave myself the space to relax and be, which in this particular case was what I truly needed, and from there could find more space and motivation to continue and move forward with life.

Get to What's Below The Surface: Transformational Kinesiology

My work with Transformational Kinesiology (TK) is the most powerful tool I've found for identifying what's behind my experiences and getting to the underlying or root cause. I chose to pursue this work because I was perpetually amazed at how different I could feel in the course of just one session. Multiple times I have literally felt like I got my life back. I have gone from feeling contracted, discouraged or depressed to feeling energized, motivated, and empowered, and I have repeatedly witnessed clients recover themselves in much the same way.

In one particularly memorable session, Jenny came to me after having felt out of sorts for quite some time, maybe a month or more, and she just could not seem to shake the heavy and depressed feelings. What we uncovered through that session stuck with me. (In this work we hold space for the possibility that we have lived many lives, and that other lives can have significant impact on this one. If that doesn't fit with how you see the world, working with the imagery we access, whether or not you believe it is what happened to you in some other life time, can create powerful shifts and changes in your state of being.) In the lifetime I accessed with Jenny, she was locked at the bottom of a tower. There was a ladder up the inside of the tower to a window at the top. If she climbed up the ladder and out the window, she'd escape being locked in the tower, but she would also fall to her death. She had a strong sense of "damned if I do, damned if I don't" that tied directly into what was going on in her present life at that time.

Once she identified and understood the subconscious beliefs and patterns associated with that life and how they were outdated and no longer served her, it was truly like she had returned to the land of the living and had energy and vitality for life again. I have witnessed this shift in clients over and over again, and I cannot even count how many times this has happened for me. Even in the process of writing this book, I've gotten stuck and twisted up in places and totally transformed them through a TK session. It never ceases to amaze me. I'm thoroughly convinced that when we can understand what's going on for us at the core, then we have the power to change it, or perhaps more accurately, our perspective changes and it changes on its own.

How do you go about applying this to yourself and your own life in a way that can be liberating? Start by getting curious and asking questions. As you do, remember that what is true for you will make you feel lighter, a lie will make you feel heavier. You're looking for what creates shift, expansion, or lightness in your life.

Use Questions to Create Shifts in Your Reality

Here are some questions you can use to start creating shifts in your reality:

- What am I aware of here that I have not been acknowledging?

- Is this even mine? (More about this in the next chapter.)

- What could this be telling me about myself and my experience?

- What am I feeling right now, and what needs could those feelings be pointing to?

- What wisdom, insight or information about myself or life can this experience provide?

Just ask the questions. Don't go looking for the answers through your cognitive abilities. Be open to seeing what insights, information or impressions emerge. Perhaps you get an instant picture or the situation just feels lighter. Ideas or words could form in your head. This is a very different space from trying to figure out the answer. When you are engaging your cognitive mind and trying to figure something out, you are basically just rearranging over and over again all the information that you already have. There is little space to receive or perceive new information or new possibilities. What we're after with these questions is creating space for those possibilities, and it's a lot more like just wondering. Employ curiosity, truly wonder, be open to receiving. What different information and possibilities can show up in your life? If you like, you can go for a walk and just let whatever comes to you come, or you can sit in quiet meditation or contemplation and see what is revealed in that way.

Use Your Feelings to Help You Find Your Needs

Another exercise you can use is to identify your feelings and connect them with whatever needs they might be indicating. (Before you do this, please be sure to ask yourself if what you're feeling and experiencing is actually yours, because if it is just awareness, then this exercise will not work all that well. I'll talk more about that in the next chapter.)

Sometimes we confuse needs with strategies. A strategy is specific; a need is universal. If I need you to respect me more, I have tied my need for respect with the strategy of how you engage with me. I might choose to not spend time with someone because it doesn't line up with what I experience as respect, but I can still get that need for respect met elsewhere. Don't give your power away. If you separate your needs from specific strategies to have those needs met, you'll have so many more options for supporting your well-being.

Below is an exercise to help you start to connect your feelings and your needs.

Connect Your Feelings with Your Needs

You can use this sentence structure to help you:

In this moment I am aware that I am feeling _____ and it is pointing me to a need for_____.

Here are some examples of what it might look like:

- In this moment I am feeling grouchy and it is pointing me to the need for space.

- In this moment I am feeling sad and it is pointing me to the need for connection

- In this moment I am feeling joyful and it is pointing me to the need for connection

There are a huge number of connections and possibilities here. Feelings can point us to needs that have not been satisfied, but they can also point us to needs fulfilled, like joy and connection in the last example. When you make these connections, what does it shift for you?

Once you have identified what is behind your feeling you may already feel differently, or you may have more self-awareness and ability to identify some ways that you can successfully tend to yourself and your well-being. If you're particularly upset by something external in your life, like something that someone did or said that you're not happy with, it can be very tempting to engage your judgments and your story. *"What a jerk." "How inconsiderate." "That person is so rude."* Yet, if you can connect what needs are behind those judgments, you will more quickly be able to move from your irritation to taking care of your needs. Can you translate what feelings and needs might be behind the statements made above?

For more on this topic, check out *Nonviolent Communication* by Marshall Rosenberg, or attend a nonviolent communication workshop. This is a far more extensive body of work than I can possibly even indicate here, and there are a huge number of books, classes, and other resources available for learning. The goal here is to give you the basic understanding of the relationship between feelings and needs and to help you start to connect with what's going on inside of you. Can you begin to see how your feelings might serve a purpose and be pointing you toward your needs?

Chapter Six
Awareness is (Almost) Everything

*"em·path: noun
A person thought to have the ability to perceive or
experience the emotional state of another individual."*

AMERICAN HERITAGE DICTIONARY, 5TH EDITION

Are You Actually Empathic
(And Not Just Really Screwed Up?)

Have you ever considered that what you're experiencing might not be yours? At first glance this seems like an absurd possibility. *Of course it's mine! I experience it, I feel it, it feels so intense, so real, what do you mean it's not mine? How is that even possible?*

Do you ever walk into a room and get a sense of the tension in that space? Can you tell there's just been a fight or an altercation even though no one is saying anything about it? That's not yours or your experience, but you can practically *feel the tension in the room?* Can you tell when your friend is upset even if she says that everything is fine? Do you ever get emotional listening to the news or hearing a story? Maybe you're moved or touched because it relates to something in you, or could it also be that you're empathizing and feeling the emotions of the people telling the story even if they aren't present?

That's a capacity you have to perceive what is going on in other people's worlds without any logical explanation. What if that capacity is far greater than you ever thought it was? What if a large percentage of what you thought was you or your issues is actually awareness? What if you're incredibly perceptive and aware of everything going on around you, but you just decided that it was you? Realizing this about myself and understanding how to work with it was a true game changer for me. I used to think I was really screwed up with a lot of social and emotional problems. I wondered why, after so many years of working on myself and trying to figure myself and my life out, I still felt so screwed up. Not always, but enough that it created challenges and problems in my life.

You Can't Fix, Solve, Heal or Resolve Something That's Not Actually Yours

Here's what I learned: You cannot fix, solve, heal, or resolve something that did not belong to you in the first place. Let me say that again. *You cannot resolve, solve, heal or fix something that didn't belong to you in the first place.* It is just awareness. There is nothing to fix. You are just aware of what is happening around you. If you perceive someone else's sadness or agitation and then try to figure out why you're sad or what you can do about it, you probably aren't going to be very successful. The one thing you can change is to acknowledge to yourself what you are aware of and to begin to perceive the difference between what is actually you and what is not. I cannot emphasize enough how huge this was for me. If you've been working on yourself for what feels like forever and it just seems like you're still plagued by unpleasant feelings, or can't quite seem to be happy, there's a very good chance that you are just perceiving the realities of others and thinking they are yours.

How do you separate out what is truly yours from that which you are just perceiving? It's as simple as just asking. For literally everything that shows up in your life and your reality, just ask, "Is this mine?" This can be a feeling, a thought, an emotion, a physical sensation, even a craving. Just ask if it is yours. If you notice that what you're experiencing shifts or feels lighter, then it probably wasn't.

I started to put this to use with some startling results. I was lying on my bed crying, tears streaming down my face, when I remembered to ask, "*Is this mine?*" The sadness lifted and the tears completely stopped. I couldn't even access or feel the sadness that just moments ago had precipitated me crying. Gone. Completely gone. Before I was introduced to this idea, I would have never even considered that the sadness I was experiencing wasn't mine. As I felt the sadness come on I attached a story and reason to my sadness that seemed perfectly relevant and logical to my life, yet when I asked that question, the sadness completely went away. "*Wow, that's pretty cool,*" I thought. "*I wonder what else I'm just perceiving that isn't even mine?*"

In the past, thinking it was my sadness, I would believe the story and reasons I created about why I was feeling sad. Then I would go about trying to fix, heal, solve, resolve the story I had created so I could finally have the happy self and life I kept on trying to find. It didn't really work very well and even if it did work at all, the next time I was aware of someone else's sadness, I'd be right back there again, wondering why I felt sad, or depressed, or anxious, or just not all that happy and why I couldn't seem to change it for any significant length of time.

How do I know that these feelings are someone else's and that they didn't just go away for some other perhaps coincidental reason? Another day, out of the blue I started to feel incredibly stressed about life. It seemed so strange because I had been feeling fine and then *boom*, here I was feeling this sense of stress about my life. Knowing it might not be mine, I wondered if I were just aware of something. I got a sense that perhaps it was connected to my friend Raphael (who lived hours away from where I was), so I sent him a text. *"Have you been feeling at all stressed lately?"* I asked.

"Yes!" was his emphatic reply.

We texted back and forth for a few moments. By the end of that exchange, the stress I'd been acutely feeling completely went away and I felt fine. Not every time I'm aware of something do I have the opportunity to have external confirmation, but I have received enough of it to know that it's not just my imagination. Sometimes I am aware of something in someone else's reality that they may not even be aware of themselves. However, I have learned to trust myself and my sense of things, because most often it shifts my experience and also gives me valuable information that helps me better relate to the other person or can also help that person in some way.

Acknowledging that I'm empathic and incredibly aware, and learning to work with it has given me an entirely different understanding of myself and my experience of life. I can honestly say that most of the time I feel sane and happy. Many times I see friends or acquaintances going through some sort of emotional turmoil and it is often clear to me that what's going on for them is the activation of their empathic abilities that they haven't yet recognized they have. I wish they knew what it took me nearly two decades of my life and incredible amounts of anguish, pain, and suffering to discover. I can imagine what a different life I would have had and how much pain and suffering it could have saved me if I'd only gotten this information sooner.

Could You Be Incredibly Empathic Too?

- Do you feel easily affected by the people around you?

- Do you have moods and emotions that seem to come out of nowhere and just as suddenly lift?

- Is it often hard to be in large groups of people or do you wonder why you find it so hard to be around certain people?

- Do you just feel weird and different, like maybe you're from some alien planet and there's just something everyone else knows that you can't quite figure out?

- Does it feel sometimes like a cloud is hanging over you and it just follows you around no matter what you do or where you go?

- Do you have lots of weird feelings and emotions you don't quite understand?

- When someone tells you an emotional or graphic story, do you feel it yourself?

- Are romantic relationships challenging for you and do you feel like you don't get what's going on?

- Does being around certain people bring up strong emotions that you don't really understand?

- Do you cry or get overwhelmed by emotion at times when you're listening to the news?

These are all experiences that could easily be the result of being an empathic person.

If you're going about your day or walking down the street and all of a sudden your mood shifts or you start to feel upset about your life when you were feeling fine before, there's a very good chance that what just showed up is actually awareness. I've had days when, all of a sudden, I start feeling funky or unhappy in some way. I'll start worrying about something that wasn't bothering me before or feel upset about something that wasn't upsetting me. Or I'll just get a weird and heavy feeling or mood and I won't know why I'm no longer feeling okay. I'll try to figure out what's going on or why I'm so unhappy, but without coming to any resolution or insight the feeling will just lift and go away. Weird, right? Well, what if experiences like this are actually you being aware of someone or something? Maybe you just walked by someone on the street who was super worried and stressed out and, *bam*, you're feeling it and taking it on as you!

What If the Crazy Thoughts in Your Head Aren't Yours?

It's not just with feelings, either. Do you ever have crazy thoughts that you wonder where they come from? Does the chatter in your head just seem incessant and at times more than a little crazy-making? Could it be that you're actually extremely aware of the thoughts of the people around you? Not necessarily just the people that are in your physical presence, but the people in proximity, like the house next door, in your building, or throughout your town. How much of that mental activity and insanity is really yours? Again, if you are used to thinking every single thing you perceive is yours, then this may seem like a pretty radical idea, but what if it is true?

What happens for you when you spend time in nature? Do you feel the same amount of mental chatter and stirred-up emotions, or does something different happen? Do you start to feel more space in your head, more ease in your body? Do you begin to relax and feel your stress and troubles melt away? While nature in and of itself may have a soothing effect on mind and body, could it also be that the space you have taken away from other people, their emotions, and their thoughts has created more space and peace for you?

I was speaking to a woman who called in on the crisis line at the shelter where I work. She was quite upset, questioning her perceptions of reality, and wondering if maybe she was just crazy, even though she didn't think she really was. I assured her that I was pretty sure she wasn't and that she was just super empathic and aware. I asked her, *"When you get away from people, when you go out in nature, do you feel insane and crazy anymore?"* She immediately recognized that when she is in nature and not around people and all of their crazy thoughts and points of view, she feels very different: more herself, more sane. This can also be true when you are alone with you. If taking time away from people and being by yourself feels better than being with them, especially when there's not something you can point to about them that is challenging for you, there's a good chance you are picking up on their energy empathically. Maybe all those crazy thoughts and feelings are awareness that you haven't yet learned to work with.

Learn to Identify What's Truly Yours

What could your life be like if you could easily and quickly identify what is yours and what you're just aware of? What if you could find that same ease, peace and space you have in nature, even when you're in the middle of a group of people or just going about your day?

Since discovering these tools and learning to identify what is truly me from what is not me, my life has vastly improved. I am so much happier than I have ever been and it's so much easier for me to socialize or be around people. I have a freedom and lightness to my being I didn't know was possible.

Learning to identify what is yours and what is not is a majorly important cornerstone and first step on this journey. If you're still getting mixed up with what is yours and what's not, you'll be trying to fix, solve, heal or resolve things that don't belong to you, and it will seem like all the other things you're doing just don't work. One way to get a sense of what is truly you is to question all of your thoughts, feelings, emotions, sensations, cravings, desires, perspectives and points of view for the next three days. Every time one shows up, just ask, "is this mine?" If it shifts, goes away, gets lighter, or changes for you in any way, then it didn't belong to you in the first place. It was just something you were perceiving or aware of. (Even if it doesn't shift, it may still not be yours, but we'll address that more in future chapters.)

You don't have to know whose it is, though sometimes you will. Just know that if it shifts and changes for you, it wasn't actually yours. Do this for three days for *every* thought, feeling, emotion and sensation you can possibly remember to ask this for. Why? Because if you do, it will give you the incredible connection to the space, ease and peace of you akin to what you might experience in nature. You will start to comprehend just how much you take on as your own that isn't and perhaps for the first time you will start to be aware of what it feels like to just be you.

If this feels confusing to you or if you can't tell if things are shifting or making a difference, I have another tool for you. Have you ever heard of kinesiology or muscle testing? (Yes, I mentioned it before but didn't fully explain what it is.) It's a way to work with the muscles of the body to gain all sorts of information. Many folks are familiar with kinesiology for testing food sensitivities and allergies, which is one of the many ways it can be applied. In my work and in this book, we will use it as a tool to help you understand what is true for you at a whole-being level, not just with your conscious mind. We will also use it to help you access those hidden and subconscious layers of your being that may be contributing to some of the places you continue to feel stuck or challenged in your life.

Basic Kinesiology for You and Your Well-Being

There are many ways to muscle test, some probably best taught in the classroom and not a book, and some are easier to do on yourself than others. For right now I'm going to teach you a very simple muscle test that you can easily use for yourself. Are you ready?

Stand up.

Find a comfortable stance with your feet no more than hip-width apart.

Relax your shoulders and your body and find your standing center.

Now, bring your hands together like you're opening and reading a book, pinky fingers touching.

Keeping your hands in the open book position, tap the sides of the palms just below your pinky fingers together. If you're sensitive, you'll notice that this has an effect on your body. But if you don't notice anything, that's fine too. This is just helping to balance your system before we do the actual test.

Now we are ready to test.

The easiest first test is just to pick up something you're considering eating. Take an apple for example. Hold the apple in your hands at about chest height. Stay in your relaxed stance and notice if your body wants to fall forward or lean back or if it just stays neutral. This is your indicator. If you move toward something, you're attracted to it, if you move back, the opposite is true.

This can also be considered a yes or a no.

Now let's try a mental question.

Take your same relaxed stance.

Tap the sides of your hands together.

Bring something into your awareness and ask, "Is this mine?"

See which way your body wants to go.

This is just a way to help you more deeply connect with your own internal knowing, to move beyond second-guessing yourself and to help you understand what's true for you.

If you find this helpful, there are many ways you can use this process that will help you train your awareness and get a sense of what's yours and what's not, what's true for you and what isn't. For now, you can just use it with the "Is this mine?" exercise to help you separate out what's you and what's not you.

Chapter Seven
Know You and Your Own Energy

*"I want to know if you can disappoint another
to be true to yourself, if you can bear the accusation
of betrayal and not betray your own soul."*

ORIAH MOUNTAIN DREAMER

Fitting in to Other People's Realities

I have noticed some common behaviors and experiences that many of my clients share that are directly linked to their empathic nature, whether or not they have realized that they are empathic. Empaths have a tendency to disappear. What do I mean by that? They shift and adjust themselves to accommodate everyone else until they practically don't exist anymore. They lose touch with their own energy, perspectives and desires, and just merge into everyone else until they don't know where they end and the other person begins. This can ultimately create a lot of challenge and suffering.

When you're empathic, you can feel acutely what is happening in the people around you, and because it can feel intense or uncomfortable, adjusting yourself to accommodate the needs and feelings of others can seem like the most natural and logical thing to do. When they are happy, then you can be happy, or so you subconsciously think. If you just tend to them and what's going on for them, then you won't have to feel it so much.

Many of us are not conscious that this is what we are doing, and it can happen almost automatically. Chances are you are a very great shape shifter. You know how to accommodate others, to make yourself agreeable, to give other people what they desire, and not to take or ask for too much for yourself. How much do you shrink, change, or make yourself small so as not to upset others and their realities? Have you figured out how to adjust and meld yourself to any given situation in a way that will maintain the most peace and harmony for the people around you?

I'm guessing you also have a lot of compassion and care for other people's suffering and you'll go out of your way to help. It's hard to see someone struggling or in distress and not feel obliged to do something about it. Caring deeply for others and having compassion for their suffering can be a wonderful thing. Most of the time, however, I see this happening at the expense of the caring person.

How much of your life have you spent in one way or another responding to or taking care of other people's needs? Do you give and give and give and at the end of the day do you just feel drained and like there is nothing left for you? Despite how much you extend yourself and show up for others, when it comes down to it, are there very few people that would actually show up for you? It can get exhausting and feel so confusing.

What Does It Cost You to Take Care of Everybody Else?

This kind of always caring for others dynamic started to dearly cost me. It cost me in my sense of value and self-confidence, but also energetically. I'd show up for people who were going through challenges or hurting and I would try to help them. I didn't want to abandon them in their time of need, so I would keep stretching and giving and, in their place of need and sometimes desperation, they would keep on taking. I would give and give and give until I was so spent that I couldn't go on anymore and would fall apart emotionally. I would want someone to be there for me, to support me—but since I'd set up the relationship in a way that involved me being the helper and caretaker, when I had exhausted my giving, the relationship didn't work anymore or often even exist.

As I was becoming more aware of this dynamic in my life, I noticed a particular pattern: I'd start to feel like my life was falling apart and that I was struggling and then I'd realize that it wasn't me that was feeling challenged or struggling at all. If I took just a little bit of time to disentangle myself from everyone else, I could see that I was doing fine. I'd just surrounded myself with people who I was trying to help who were going through difficult times and it was starting to wear on me and drain my energy.

Could your empathy and compassion for others be destroying your own life? Do you find yourself in relationships and situations where you're trying to support or assist people but it's actually draining you?

You can't save someone else if it is sinking your own ship in the process. What would it look like if you put *you* back into the equation of your life? What if you considered yourself, your feelings, your experiences, just as much as you have come to consider everyone else?

Putting You Back in the Equation of Your Life

Many of my clients think that to say no or to not show up for someone who is going through a hard time means they are being a mean or selfish person. How kind is it, though, to show up for someone or be friends with them because you feel sorry for them? Have you ever had someone in your life who is doing things for you or contributing to you but it is costing them? How does it feel to receive that? I realized at some point that there were people in my life that I was choosing because I felt sorry for them and wanted to help them, not because I genuinely enjoyed my relationship with them. Not only was it not contributing to me, I realized that it wasn't exactly kind to them either. Who wants to have "friends" in their lives that are only there because they feel sorry for them or are trying to fix them?

It was a glorious day when I realized I didn't have to like or be friends with everyone, when I discovered I could choose what I wanted and walk away from the things, people, and conditions that were draining my energy and didn't feel like a contribution to my life... and it didn't make me a bad or hateful person. At a particularly low point in my life, I was deeply struggling with my relationships with other people, and so many of the encounters I had felt so weird and off. Then I spent a weekend in a cabin in the woods by myself, and was amazed at how much better I felt about myself. Living in a small rural town where I didn't really know anyone, I'd been feeling lonely and isolated, and was trying so hard to connect with people that maybe I didn't relate with that well. I declared to myself that I would rather spend the rest of my life by myself than spend one more minute in crappy-feeling social engagements. I made a choice to stop participating in dynamics and relationships that didn't feel good to me, and my quality of life immediately improved. When my self-esteem or quality of life seems to be taking a dip, I revisit this, taking a look at the relationships in my life and how I'm feeling about them. If there are any that don't feel great or are draining my energy, I make adjustments to how or with whom I'm relating, and I almost inevitably feel better.

One of the most critical things I have recognized, both from personal experience and also from the majority of my clients, is the importance of putting yourself back into the center of your own life. For me, this has meant choosing what I want before I make accommodations and considerations for everyone else. It has meant paying attention to my desires, needs, and preferences, and making the choices that truly work for me, not just what will work for other people. After all it's my life, and I'm the one that has to live with it! What if you stopped giving up you to accommodate everyone else? I know that might seem like you're being selfish, but if you give up yourself for someone else, what do you have left? What if you were willing to choose what works for you and fully included yourself in your life?

For the next week, I have a challenge for you:

I challenge you to put yourself back into the center of your life!

Walk away from relationships or situations that drain your energy.

Choose what *you* want and what contributes to you before you consider everybody else. Make yourself, your needs, and your well-being your priority, and just for this one week, give up taking care of everybody else.

What follows are several more practices and exercises that will help you come back to you and your own energy and disentangle yourself from everybody else. Doing this has been so crucial for me and maintaining my well-being.

Reclaim Your Energy for Yourself

1. Choose Who You Spend Your Time with

Does your mood or feeling change when you're around certain people? Did you just think it was you? Start to notice how you feel around certain people and in certain environments. If you feel one way and then suddenly feel something different when you get around a particular person or in a particular situation, there's a good chance that it's not just that you have "social issues," but that you're actually aware of something. Sometimes limiting contact with people or situations that have a negative energetic effect on you, even if you have no rational explanation or justification why, can be incredibly empowering. (No, you're not being mean and there's not something wrong with you.) If it makes you feel better to limit contact or engagement with someone, then why not choose it? After all, it is your energy and your life!

Use the other tools in this book to help you to understand and address what you perceive, and know that it's not just because "you're moody." You might actually be aware of something, and if you learn to listen and to acknowledge your awareness, you will increase your intuitive capacities and perceptive abilities.

A few years ago I made a new friend. We seemed to relate fairly well, care about some of the same things, and have many common interests. Yet, every time I was with her I would get all these funky feelings, and when I was not with her I would go back to feeling fine. I realized that I was aware of something going on with her that I was taking on and trying to process as if it were mine. The issue didn't immediately resolve itself. I remember making notes to myself to limit my contact with her (even though I liked her) until I could better understand what was going on or how I could be with her and not take on her energy or have it bring me down. Our relationship did eventually shift and we were able to become good friends.

2. Take Time out to be with Yourself and in Your Own Energy

As a sensitive person I have found this to be incredibly important. It can be very easy to get wrapped up in other people's energy, points of view, and realities without even realizing it—even if you like them and enjoy their company and want to be spending time with them. After years of getting tangled up with others and their realities and then hitting some sort of emotional crisis or breakdown, I've learned that, if I can just take some time out to reconnect with myself and my own energy, I can feel sane and grounded again. Have you ever noticed that you feel much better after removing yourself from a particular situation or spending a couple of hours alone? What if you could start to recognize early-on when you're not sufficiently self-connected, and take a little time to re-group and find your center? This could be as little as excusing yourself during a social function and taking five minutes to self-connect, or it could be as big as spending a day or a week by yourself. If you learn to create the time and space to stay connected with yourself, I know it will make a huge difference, increase your effectiveness, and keep you feeling empowered in your life.

Even as recently as the time of writing this, I am again learning this lesson for myself. I had been pushing myself to go, go, go, taking on extra work, writing as much as I could, and not wanting to miss out on fun activities and adventures. I live in the land of outdoor adventure, so every spare moment is an opportunity to get out and do something fun and exciting. From a distance it seems like the people around me live these amazing adventure-filled lives and I don't want to miss out or be left behind. That has meant not taking time out by and for myself that I need.

After a busy week, I took a five-day trip with a friend to three national parks in our area. It was amazing and beautiful, but I felt out of sorts and not at peace a lot of the time. We even had a couple of challenging moments between us. In the back of my mind, I knew that we probably wouldn't be having the same issues if I'd taken the time to get away and be with myself for a while. The day after coming back from the trip, I woke up still feeling incredibly out of sorts. This time I finally listened and recognized that what I truly needed was just the time and space to re-connect with myself and be alone with me. By doing that, so much of the angst and agitation I'd been feeling melted away, and I came back to feeling good and positive again.

3. Expand Your Energy

What happens when you put a drop of ink in a glass of water? The water turns the color of the ink, right? What happens when you put a drop of ink in the ocean? Nothing of consequence. If you're feeling easily impacted or affected by what's going on around you, you may need to make yourself bigger and fill up more space. If you're being as big as a glass of water, then pretty much everything is going to affect you and you are going to feel it intensely. If you're being as big as the ocean, however, then most things are going to be insignificant and not have a noticeable effect on you or your well-being. Which would you rather choose?

Here's an exercise for expanding your energy so you are less impacted by whatever is happening around you. If something in particular is impacting you, think for a moment of the thing or experience before you do this exercise.

Take a moment to connect with yourself and your own body. Make adjustments to increase your comfort. You can do this in any position, but the more you can relax (without falling asleep) the better.

Notice your breath. See if you can relax into yourself a little bit more.

Now see if you can get a sense of the energy that runs through your body, that is the energy of you.

Once you have a sense of that energy, see if you can expand that energy out from your body an inch in every direction.

Now let's go for a foot in every direction: above you, below you, in front of you, and behind you.

Are you still aware of yourself and your energy?

Now let's see if you can expand that out six feet in every direction.

Now let's fill up the room or space you are in.

Now see if you can expand your energy to fill up your town.

How about the region in which you live?

Keep expanding out your energy. Can you expand it out to fill up the whole country?

The whole continent?

Expand your energy out to fill up the whole planet.

Now expand it out into our Milky Way galaxy.

And beyond, into other galaxies and into the universe of the infinite.

Notice how you are feeling.

Do you feel any different now?

Can you feel that expanded and expansive energy which is you?

What happened to the thing that was impacting you? Do you relate to it differently, does it impact you differently now?

Stay connected to this space, this expansion, and this energy.

Invite the entire universe to contribute to you and support you.

Now slowly bring your awareness back into this galaxy.

Back to planet Earth.

Back to the continent where you are.

Keeping your energy expanded, bring your awareness back to the country where you are.

Back to the area, back to the town.

Back to the specific location, and back to your own body.

How do you feel now?

How do you relate with or experience the thing that was impacting you?

As I write this, I feel the impact of this exercise on my being and how my energy shifts and changes. I am amazed at how, when I take the time to do the exercise, I experience a significant change in my state of being. If you just read through the exercise and didn't actually do it, I highly recommend going back through and doing it. Sometimes I tell myself I need to expand my energy and make myself bigger, but without going through the actual process. Sometimes that does work, but often times it takes fully doing the exercise to make the significant change in my state of being.

4. Pull Your Energy Back to You

Another exercise I've found incredibly helpful is to imagine pulling all of my energy back to me. I imagine this like threads or strings going out in every direction, and I just reel them in and pull them back to me. Maybe your energy is hooked in with another person or situation. It could be that you're just feeling them or are worried or concerned about them, or maybe you're entangled with them and their energy in some other way. Just imagine unhooking and pulling all of that energy back you. I think of a fishing rod with hooks. I take out the hooks wherever they are and just reel the line back in to me. You can also imagine that you are like a giant bowl. I think of spaghetti spilling over the sides. I want to put all of the spaghetti back into the bowl, have all of my energy in my bowl and fill up the bowl with my own energy.

This practice came to me as I became aware of just how much I was mixed up with other people's energies and their realities. I would sit on my bed and just focus on retrieving my energy and disentangling it from everyone else. I noticed an incredible improvement in my state of being. You don't have to know exactly where your energy is tangled up to have this work, it's enough just to unhook and pull it back to you.

This can go the opposite way too. Sometimes I get the sense that other people are energetically hooked into me and may be draining my energy. In this case, I imagine unhooking or unplugging them from me and sending all their threads back to them so that I can be free. Sometimes it will be enough just to visualize disconnecting or removing their energy from your space, or removing yourself from theirs. Other times there may be underlying reasons that you are still entangled or unable to disconnect, and that may require further understanding before you can be free.

5. Fill Yourself Up with Your Own Energy

Something I've started to notice is that the more I'm engaged in doing my own thing and showing up for my own life, the less I am impacted by everybody else. The more you show up and fill up your own life with you, the less space there is for everybody else to occupy the space of you. Sometimes I'll feel weird, off, or twisted up in some way before I need to show up for something like a client call, presentation, interview, or a speech. I can't tell you how many times it happens that when I show up for that thing and connect with my competence, those feelings just completely go away. When I engage with my life in a bigger way, all the little things that are impacting me and pulling at my energy just go away. The more I focus on the things I'm doing and take care of my own life rather than trying to take care of everyone and everything else, I inevitably feel better.

6. Ask Questions and Follow Your Awareness

This is a theme I talk about throughout the book, but it is worth mentioning again here. Questions are powerful tools for awareness. When you ask questions you can access more information than with your cognitive thoughts and your conclusions. The questions I'm talking about are a sort of wondering without needing to have an answer and just seeing what shows up as a result. Maybe you ask a question and everything gets lighter... perhaps you get an idea or some other form of inspiration, or maybe something just shifts for you and you feel better. If something shifts or gets lighter for you, there's a good chance you got what was true for you in that moment.

Let's say you have this nagging feeling that just won't leave you alone. What if you started asking some questions? Questions like, "What am I aware of here?" Maybe you notice that you're aware of someone in your life. What's going on with that person? Does he need anything from me? Is there a way I can contribute? These can all be useful questions. Notice what changes you experience or what makes it feel lighter. Move in that direction, and it will help to create more ease for you. What's true for you will make you feel lighter, what's a lie for you will make you feel heavier.

I was out for a walk with my friend Amy and she was struggling in a relationship to one of our other friends. She is incredibly empathic and she said, *"I hate it; I hate how sensitive I am. I wish it would just go away."* I felt sad to hear that, because I know that being sensitive can be an incredible gift and capacity if you can learn to work with it. I shared that with her, and I asked her what she was aware of in that moment. She was aware that she was feeling the reality of this particular friend. I asked her if there was anything she could do or if the friend needed anything from her. She got the sense that she could send loving and supportive energy to that friend. She did it in her own way, and noticed that it did make things lighter and easier for her.

If something is showing up in your life, some energy and experience, ask questions, see if you can understand what it is, and what is required of you in relationship to it. So often I've had weird feelings or experiences, and through inquiry I've been able to identify who they are connected to and how they relate to me. Sometimes just acknowledgment of my awareness is sufficient, sometimes something more is required. Maybe I need to text or call them or send them energy. Maybe I need to understand something about the situation. My experience has been that, when I get to the core of what is going on, the experience significantly shifts for me.

Chapter Eight
Why Therapy Might Not Be Working for You and What You Can Do About It

*"If you don't ask the right questions,
every answer turns up wrong."*

Ani DiFranco

Have you tried therapy? Has it worked for you? My guess is that if you're still reading this book, then, you've been to therapy but you didn't find it all that helpful; the whole premise and model of therapy doesn't feel right for you and you haven't bothered to try it; or therapy worked for you for a time but you have outgrown it or find it is no longer providing the help or support you need. I've had a few different therapists that I worked with for more than a few sessions and several that didn't last for any length of time.

There were things that were certainly helpful about therapy, but it didn't significantly change the experiences of my life. Reflecting back, I better understand now why the therapy model, which can at times be very helpful and is truly the right fit for some people, is also often limited in what it can provide. If therapy hasn't really worked for you, here is some of what you may be missing:

Take Your Empathic Capacities into Account

One thing that can limit the effectiveness of therapy is that you can't fix, heal, solve, or resolve what didn't belong to you in the first place. If you're going to therapy to fix "your problems" but a big piece of what's creating that experience for you is that you're super aware of other people's realities, then therapy probably isn't going to work all that well. Almost every approach to emotional healing that I've encountered (and there are many!) automatically assumes that what is going on for you is your problem and something in you that needs fixing or healing. Seldom is there acknowledgment that you might just be incredibly aware or empathic!

During all those years I spent thinking I was so screwed up and trying to "work on my stuff" and heal myself, I got very skilled at handling my emotions and experiences, but it didn't fundamentally change what I was experiencing. I just had better coping skills. No matter how much I explored my own psyche, I couldn't seem to move beyond my funky emotional states and my experiences with depression. This was, of course, in part because I was incredibly empathic and aware of what was going on around me but I didn't know it at the time. No one else, including all the healers and alternative practitioners I went to for support and guidance, knew it either, at least not to the degree that it was happening for me. Once I learned to identify the difference between what is my experience and what I'm just aware of, my whole life began to change. The places that I once thought I was the most screwed up have turned out to be some of my greatest gifts and capacities. Telling someone that what you're experiencing belongs to other people or the thoughts in your head aren't even yours, could mean being labeled you with some sort of mental health disorder. How ironic that what helped me finally feel sane was to acknowledge something for which other people might label me crazy. If it's crazy, I'll take it, because I finally feel sane and am able to engage with and function in life more successfully than I ever have before.

Include the Subconscious

Much of what creates our experiences and our behavior is subconscious. It is, therefore, difficult to identify or transform through traditional methods of therapy or personal development. The subconscious is often thought of as this dark, murky, self-sabotaging, and not fully understood place in the psyche. However, in my work transforming subconscious beliefs and patterns, I've come to see it more simply: The subconscious is where we put all of the information we don't want to have to re-evaluate or think about every day. It's like a computer program we've set up to handle the bulk of our interactions so we don't have to manually process each one. The only problem with this is that it's often based on outdated information. Our automatic responses may still be coming from when we were five! Most therapies don't adequately address these underlying beliefs and patterns, and as a result have limited effectiveness. You can learn new skills and gain self-understanding, but if it's only at the conscious level and your subconscious is not provided with new strategies to handle a given situation, you're probably not getting the kinds of results you would like. It is through understanding these subconscious layers that I am able to see that there is a reason or purpose behind everything I experience, and that I do truly work.

Gaining access to what was going on for me at the subconscious level was like being given the key to the treasure chest of myself. All I knew before was that I felt bad. I didn't know why, I didn't know exactly what was upsetting me or why I couldn't just get over it. I didn't know why all of my consciousness and intellectual understanding weren't changing my lived experience. When I discovered Transformational Kinesiology it gave me access to parts of myself that I just couldn't see before. It helped me understand myself, my experience, and my life at a much deeper and entirely different level. Not only was I able to see and identify the subconscious patterns that were continuing to run my life, I could also see how and why they were created and that they were designed to help me but that they might no longer be serving me and transform them or let them go. Being able to identify what was going on below the surface was one of my first keys to unlocking myself from depression and finding happiness and emotional freedom in my life.

Here's an example of how a subconscious patterning process might work: You're a little girl, you depend on your parents for your very survival. There are certain things your parents have decided are okay to say or believe, and certain things they've decided are not. If you say the right things you'll be okay, but if you disagree, you'll encounter your parents' wrath, which as a small child who needs their parents to survive, is akin to facing death. In all of your wisdom and intelligence you recognize that it's not safe to speak your mind, and at five years old you make a firm decision, probably somewhere subconsciously, to keep your opinions to yourself. Given the context, that could be a very smart, self-preserving decision. This information gets filed away in your subconscious, "*It's not safe to speak my mind. I'm going to keep my opinions to myself,*" and continues to run in the background of your life.

You grow up, your life conditions and circumstances have changed. Saying what you think doesn't have such dire consequences, yet whenever you go to express your ideas or opinions, it feels pretty scary and very difficult to express your own ideas. Still running your life is the idea that it's not safe to speak your mind and that you must keep your opinions to yourself. Until you can go back and look at that belief, see that those are decisions and conclusions you made for very good reasons, and that now circumstances have changed and you choose something different, it will remain subconscious and will continue to fuel your reactions and be more powerful than your conscious awareness.

If you've been trying to figure out what your problem is, or create change for yourself for a long time, and just seem to be spinning in circles or not getting very far, there's a good chance that you're missing what's at the real heart of your experience. There is so much more to your experiences than what you're aware of with your conscious mind. Most therapy is only able to address what you're consciously aware of and not the deeper layers that are what create your experiences and behaviors. I found it incredibly empowering and helpful for me to be able to identify and see what is truly going on at the subconscious level. Many approaches that work with the subconscious mind just work with subliminal reprogramming, not necessarily helping you see and understand your subconscious beliefs, patterns, and motivations. The TK process gives access to seeing and understanding these deeper layers like nothing else I have ever experienced, and brings about a level of shift and transformation, not to mention self-awareness, that can be truly liberating.

Even now, when I feel stuck with something I don't understand or cannot change, I seek support through the TK process. So many times I have thought, "*Oh, this time I am just broken, screwed up or truly depressed,*" only to have a TK session that reveals what's really been going on for me. Once I get to the core, it feels like I just got myself and my life back. Both with myself or with my clients, I'll think, "*Oh, this time the process is not going to work,*" but every time it does, and there is a noticeable shift toward greater well-being.

Creating What You Desire vs. Focusing on What's Wrong

Unlike a process like TK, which is focused on where you want to go or what you want to create, a lot of conventional approaches to healing–and particularly conventional therapy–focus on what's wrong or broken that needs fixing. The bulk of the focus or energy goes to the problem. As a result, you have a lot of understanding and awareness about your problems, why or how you are broken, maybe even lots of labels for your experience, but not necessarily what's required to make a change and take you to some different place in your life. Trying to figure out what's wrong with you can be like getting caught in a maze to which there is no solution and where you just keep going around and around and around.

I was caught in this maze when, in a particular moment I clearly saw the insanity of trying to figure myself out in this way. I decided to just stop. I have an image of this little figurine of myself lost and wandering through the maze, being picked up out of the maze by this big hand that places me somewhere else. What if it honestly is that easy? From that point on, I shifted my focus and energy to what I wished to have and create, and to believe in my basic functionality and goodness. How would your life be different if you operated from the premise that you're basically functional and good, rather than that you're broken, screwed up, or in need of fixing?

It is my view that the goal of any type of healing or self-exploration process should be toward empowerment and feeling more competent and better about yourself. If what you're doing does not contribute to your sense of empowerment, then you're probably not on the right track. If you feel worse and not better about yourself as a result of therapy or any other modality, then something isn't right. Remember, what's true for you will feel light, not heavy. My friend Clara shared with me that her therapist told her she had all these problems, like relationship addiction and I can't remember what else. Believing this information, I watched her shrivel and wilt. It just made her more depressed and feel worse about herself. There's a time and a place for healing old wounds or hurt places, or even recognizing one's own dysfunctional patterns, but it can be done in a way that feels truly healing and empowering and helps you make forward movement in your life, not just feel worse about yourself.

The Client-Therapist Relationship

Whether or not it's conscious, in a client-therapist relationship it can be easy to avoid or omit certain things that you don't want to talk about. Have you ever had the experience that a therapist (or other type of practitioner) isn't getting you, or worse yet, steering you in a direction that doesn't feel right or true for you? So much of what happens in therapy is dependent on—and easily determined or manipulated by—the client-therapist relationship. It can take a lot of time to build trust, safety, and rapport before it is safe to talk about the things that truly matter and even longer before you see a shift and a difference in your experience. The nature of the relationship and the way it is set up is also hierarchical, which can make it difficult to experience full empowerment. The therapist is always the one assumed to have the superior knowledge, experience, or wisdom. What do you do when you realize you are more aware of yourself and what's going on for you than they are? When you have a better understanding or are more conscious, it can set up a challenging dynamic.

One of the things I absolutely love–both as a client and a practitioner–about TK is that it introduces a third element of muscle testing into the process. It cannot be as easily manipulated nor is so dependent on the relationship or the personality of either person. It also provides a mechanism to very quickly and easily pinpoint the core issues and to identify exactly what needs to be addressed within a session.

I was volunteering at a free health clinic when I had a young woman who I'll call Sophie come in for a session. She said, "*I'd like to focus on this or on this.*" (I can't remember the specific topics.) I began the basic TK process. When we muscle tested for what to focus on, I told her that her body was telling me that there was something else that would be more useful or relevant to look at. I swear, Sophie's jaw literally dropped to the floor. She got very real with me and said, "*Okay, this is what it is.*" She revealed how she'd been repeatedly raped by her father and was questioning her sanity around all of it. I was a complete stranger to her, that's not something she was just going to tell me off the bat, and yet with the TK process we were able to very quickly identify exactly what to focus on, and to create some greater sense of sanity and empowerment around the situation because of it.

Look Below the Surface

In my searching and exploration I have not found anything quite like TK, though I have found many other modalities that offer other valuable processes that supplement it. I've drawn all of these into my work with clients. Whether you choose to work with me or are drawn to work with someone else, I highly recommend work that will address what's going on at the subconscious level and not just at the surface. I scratched the surface and accumulated lots of intellectual understanding, but it only ever had limited effectiveness. The subconscious is where so many of the mystifying pieces of our experience take place. Missing that is like just tasting the icing and thinking it's the whole cake.

Aside from hiring me or someone like me, here are some basic tools and practices you can start to play around with to bring you greater insight and awareness and access what's going on for you below the surface.

Put Kinesiology to Use

For empaths it is often very easy to identify with other people and their realities. We already looked at using kinesiology to help you tell what's yours and what's not. You may also often identify with another person and their experience, or you could also be identifying with yourself in the future or the past.

Do the basic kinesiology test we set up in Chapter Six. The best way to test is not to ask questions but to make statements and to see how your body responds. You will see that I have put the following in the form of statements rather than of questions.

Helpful Kinesiology Tests:

Find your relaxed stance.

Tap the sides of your hands together (as we learned in chapter six).

Now, say to yourself, "*I am (Fill in your name) here and now.*"

If you fall forward, that's a yes, if you fall back, that's a no.

If it's a yes, you're good to go! (Don't you want to be yourself in the here and now?)

If it's a no, first say the statement, "*I am myself (or your name).*"

If it's a no and you'd like to know what or whom you are identified with, you can make statements like:

"*I am another person.*"

You might have a hunch about who you're identified with or picking up on, in which case you could say, "*I am_____ (that person's name).*"

Do you fall forward or back? Forward is a yes, back is a no.

If you have identified that you *are* yourself you can state:

"*I am myself in the future.*"

Yes or no?

"*I am myself in the past.*"

Yes or no?

You could keep going here, making more statements. If you're identifying with yourself in the past, you could find out at what age, and then go even further to identify a place or particular incident. Once I find a particular age or incident I inquire into what decisions, conclusions or beliefs I may have put into place at that time that might have relevance to something happening in my present life. If you're identified with someone else, you could find out who and explore even further with statements like:

"I'm taking on this person's stuff."

"This person is a mirror for me" (showing you something about yourself that you haven't wanted to see).

"I am resonant with this person" (there's something in you or your experience that is similar to and resonating with what that person is going through).

"There is something this person needs from me" and if so you can ask questions about what would be the greatest contribution.

However, if you just want to bring yourself back to you in the here and now, there is a simple eye rotation exercise you can do. I've found it very helpful at certain times, while at others it will help for the moment, but then I'll go back to where I was (past, future, another person) because there's something additional I need to address or look at there.

Exercise for Bringing Yourself Back to Yourself in the Here and Now:

Imagine a large circle painted in front of your face... you could see it like the edges of a larger round mirror. You are going to follow the rim of that circle with your eyes while repeating the statement: *"I am (your name), here and now."*

Move your eyes around the circle clockwise and then counterclockwise.

Move your eyes also in figure eights in both directions.

Notice if there are any places where your eyes are jumping ahead. You want to be able to move your eyes smoothly around the entire circle and through both directions of figure eights.

Once you've done that several times, once again say "*I am (your name), here and now*," and see if anything has shifted for you.

This gives you a sense of the basic muscle testing mechanism as it is used in TK and other similar kinds of work. There are many directions and applications in which this can be used that are far beyond the scope of this book. It is an incredible tool for inquiring into and discovering what is happening within your subconscious.

Many of our subconscious patterns and beliefs have their roots in experiences of childhood. In the following chapter we'll talk a lot about how the experiences of childhood could still be affecting you. This will give you some additional tools to work with and address the subconscious.

Chapter Nine

Move Beyond the Shadows of Your Childhood

"We don't yet know, above all, what the world might be like if children were to grow up without being subjected to humiliation, if parents would respect them and take them seriously as people."

ALICE MILLER

M any of our subconscious patterns and beliefs are put in place during childhood. I believe that most of us were traumatized in some way by our childhood experiences, whether we recognize it or not, and that we all have stresses and triggers related to those traumas. More and more is being learned about trauma, particularly childhood trauma and trauma that comes not just from one dramatic event but from the long-term cumulative effect of persistent small ones over time.

"Consider a birdcage. If you look very closely at just one wire in the cage, you cannot see the other wires. If your conception of what

is before you is determined by this myopic focus, you could look at that one wire, up and down the length of it, and be unable to see why a bird would not just fly around the wire any time it wanted to go somewhere. Furthermore, even if, one day at a time, you myopically inspected each wire, you still could not see why a bird would have trouble going past the wires to get anywhere. There is no physical property of any one wire, nothing that the closest scrutiny could discover, that will reveal how a bird could be inhibited or harmed by it except in the most accidental way. It is only when you step back, stop looking at the wires one by one, microscopically, and take a macroscopic view of the whole cage, that you can see why the bird does not go anywhere; and then you will see it in a moment. It will require no great subtlety of mental powers. It is perfectly obvious that the bird is surrounded by a network of systematically related barriers, no one of which would be the least hindrance to its flight, but which, by their relations to each other, are as confining as the solid walls of a dungeon."

"Oppression," in *Politics Of Reality: Essays In Feminist Theory*

So too, if you look at the realities of your own childhood or of others that you know, you can't understand what the problem was or where the trauma occurred. It does not become immediately obvious that there even *is* trauma, because no one event seems particularly alarming or upsetting. Yet what I see over and over again when I delve into what is really going on for my clients is the traumas and wounds of childhood: the frightened little girl or boy whose parents were not aware of or disregarded their needs. I see the frightened child that feels scared and uncertain that he is safe or whether there is anyone there that will take care of him. If we are willing to open our eyes, look, and truly see, we will see just how traumatic and damaging to one's psyche even many common childhood practices and "normal" childhoods have been.

Understanding the Childhood Experience

Many initial sessions with clients involve reconnecting them with that scared child part of themselves and helping them learn to identify and work with their childhood experience. I want to give you a bit of understanding and background about the dynamics and experiences that may have been present in your childhood so you can better understand them and how they might be playing out for you now, even if you're not consciously aware of their impact.

Children depend on their parents for their very survival. You will literally not survive without the support and care of your parent. Until a certain age (seven at the earliest, more commonly eight or nine), the idea that your parents could be anything less than perfect gods becomes a threat to your very existence. You need your parents to be functional and responsible, and to take care of you so that you can be okay. The possibility that they aren't is too terrifying for a little child to consider, and that child will internalize the problem rather than see their parents as anything less than perfect. If I, as a child, take on the notion that the problem is with me, then it doesn't have to be so scary or life-threatening. At least if it's me, then I can try to fix or change it—do better, be better—whatever I think will resolve the situation in my small-child logic. Then it doesn't feel like my very life is at stake and I can regain some sense of safety and power.

Children are little psychic sponges. They respond to what is happening around them, they pick up on the feelings, moods, attitudes, and issues of the adults that care for them. Just think about this for a moment: Before a child is born, they are physically a part of their mother's body. They know her intimately, feel her moods, her rhythms, everything about her. In essence they *are* her. Does it not make sense that, even after they are inhabiting an independent body, they may still know the reality of their mother without her needing to say anything? I have seen over and over again in my work with children how their actions, emotions, and behaviors are directly affected by what is going on with their parents or other caregivers. Clara came to me as she was struggling with her daughter's behavior. Clara was going through a lot, including issues around custody with her daughter Lily's father. I told her, *"Let's look at and work on what is going on with you first, and then let's see how Lily is doing."* After our first session she wrote me this message:

> *"I have to tell you that the change in my daughter since our session on Monday is nothing short of a miracle. Amazing. She is a different kid at school and is doing what I ask the first time at home. Every day I am excited to see the continued change. Thank YOU for your work, it is so important and I have been telling everyone."*

When the mother (or primary care-giver) is grounded and secure in herself, the reality of the child completely changes. As a sensitive or empathic person, this may have been even more true for you and continue to be reflected in your experiences of life. How much are you picking up on and responding or reacting to what is happening in the people around you? Quite frequently, I am reacting or responding to what is going on with others, though I haven't always been aware of it.

One day I was visiting a friend and I just got sadder and sadder until I ended up crying. When I left I felt better, and I realized I'd just been aware of something that was going on in her that she wasn't saying—by all outward appearance she seemed fine. Similarly, in another situation with a woman I'll call Beth, I just got more and more upset but I didn't know what was going on. I felt that something wasn't right but I didn't know what or why. Later, Beth revealed that she was feeling resentful toward me and that she was being energetically passive aggressive. I had been aware of it but didn't consciously know it and just felt weird and twisted up and started crying.

Childhood Trauma and Your Empathic Abilities

This is the reality for children much of the time. They are aware on the energetic level of everything that is going on around them and respond to it accordingly. You may still be doing that without even realizing it. If you've had traumatic experiences in your childhood, particularly prolonged trauma that wasn't just from one particular instance, this can be especially true. If you live in a traumatic environment and don't feel safe, your senses will become that much more heightened and you will be on constant alert, ever vigilant, in a fight-or-flight mode that stimulates the most primal areas of your brain. Through my own experiences and self-inquiry as well as with my work with clients, I've come to see the sort of sixth sense that can develop as a result of prolonged trauma. Imagine (or maybe you don't have to imagine) that you're in a family in which there is some sort of abuse taking place. As a child, that is pretty scary, but if you can know and predict when the abuse is coming, then you'll feel like you have a bit more control over the situation. Children in abusive situations will develop an almost psychic sense about the abuser so that they can know exactly what is going on for them and when the abuse is coming. They will also internalize the energy of the abuser in an attempt to understand it and also in some way resolve it, but of course that never works.

I have noticed repeatedly that when certain early childhood trauma is triggered in relationship to another person, I become acutely aware of their energy, their experiences, even their thoughts and feelings, and even when they aren't in physical proximity. At times I truly wondered if I were going crazy because it became so intense for me. I could literally feel the emotions and tap into the experience of the person who had triggered me. (It took me quite some time to identify that this is what was happening, and it could be happening for you too though you might not yet realize or recognize it.) I have been able to verify this on enough occasions that I assume it to be true the rest of the time. When I can acknowledge what I am aware of, even just to myself, it can create more ease and space in my world. Admitting that you feel others' feelings or experience their realities could be labeled as a mental health disorder, but again, it was my willingness to finally admit what I was aware of and picking up on that helped me to truly function and feel sane. If things start feeling very weird or twisted up, there's probably something you're picking up on or incredibly aware of that you haven't been acknowledging.

You in Your Family

How much was going on in your family that you were aware of, even if you didn't register it consciously? How much did you try to shift that experience for your parents? Did you try to take away their pain and suffering? And did it actually work? In a way, a family is its own unit and we each take on various different energetic roles within the family. Maybe you're the peace-maker, maybe you're the one that has all the problems. At any rate, we participate energetically with all of these dynamics, often without even realizing we are doing it.

If you're aware of something in your parents' reality, let's say their unhappiness, you might even take it on as yours and try to fix it for them so they can be happy. Whatever your parents have not resolved themselves, you may be aware of and trying to fix or resolve so that they will be present and take care of you. How much have you been trying to process and work out your parents' unresolved issues for them so that they would be available to you? For me it was my mom's unhappiness and emotional issues. In some energetic way, I tried to take them away from her so that she could finally be happy, and happy with me, and love me. Of course, that didn't work, but these kinds of dynamics and patterns that we develop through our childhood experiences continue to play out throughout our adult lives.

What Likely Happens if You Don't Resolve Your Traumas

What happens if you don't resolve your childhood traumas? If you're happy and your life is going great, then maybe you've truly put them in the past and there's nothing left there to resolve. That does not seem to be the case for most people, particularly sensitive people or empaths. Until you face and truly acknowledge, heal or resolve your childhood traumas, nothing else in your life will fully work. I wanted to get on with my life, I had big dreams for myself, I wanted to accomplish so much, and yet I kept hitting these emotional potholes. I would get to a certain place with moving forward and then something would happen that was triggering or traumatizing (whether I realized it or not), and my whole life would fall apart. I finally realized that the only way to get to a different and more fulfilling place in my life was to deal with and transform what kept on showing up for me that I hadn't wanted to acknowledge or see.

I see it with friends as well. They are going through the very same patterns where things seem to come together and then fall apart, or they just can't seem to move forward or make their lives work the way they want. It's hard for them to have a solid foundation or any real stability, to develop something in their lives that lasts. This was true for me. I never had a job for more than a year. In a span of two years I'd moved nine times before I stopped counting, and within a five year span I didn't live in any one place for more than six months, often much shorter. Within that time I was homeless more than once, including a year spent living out of my car. Resolving my traumatic experiences and conflicts of the past, particularly from childhood, has finally allowed me to move forward into a more fulfilling and settled place in life. After so many years of challenge and struggle, it's an amazing contrast and is now an experience that is truly of the past.

I can think of more than one friend who has gone through or is still going through similar patterns in their lives. Two of the people I'm thinking of have significant trauma history by anyone's standards, which neither of them have adequately resolved. Both of them have continued to try to move forward with their dreams, visions, and goals, but things perpetually don't work out. They find themselves in dysfunctional situations over and over again, often where they are being victimized or taken advantage of in some way. It is often a subconscious repetition of the original trauma from childhood that they have not been able to resolve. I feel for them, because I know and see the cycle, and know that until they truly face and heal the impacts of their original trauma, nothing in their lives is truly going to work.

It is not within the scope of this book to fully cover the dynamics and realities of healing childhood trauma and of thoroughly resolving the issues of the past. What I'm showing you here is that what's required for creating a different reality for your life is to acknowledge and work with these experiences so they no longer trip you up or run your life. If this is an area that you think you'd benefit from working with more in depth, then I recommend some personal coaching to help you transform these experiences. You are not perpetually doomed because of your past; it is possible to completely transform your experience and create a different reality for yourself, you just might need some support and guidance to do it. The tools that I offer in this chapter, regardless of what other work there is still to do, will offer you some value and benefit and help you to move forward with your life.

Who Runs The Show?

What I have seen over and over again in my work with clients is that in particular instances we get triggered, and instead of functioning as a competent adult, the inner child takes over and tries to run the show. The "inner child" is a subconscious part of you, developed through your actual childhood, and it still exists within you. It's like the little child that didn't trust her parents to take care of her, so she tries to take on the responsibility and manage things in order to survive. Her intention is to help you, but she's a little girl, so she's probably functioning from a little girl concept of reality. In my work with clients we have had some great success in learning how to identify and work with these inner children and to put the adult back in the driver's seat. It sounds funny, since these are all essentially aspects of yourself, but when you can separate out and identify which part of you is your inner child and what's the competent adult, it can make a big difference in your life. If you're unsure about who is running the show at any given moment, you can use the kinesiology exercise from the last chapter to find out.

Connect with Your Inner Child

Let me walk you through a little practice you can use to develop a relationship with the inner child part of yourself and to put your conscious adult self back into the driver's seat of your life.

The first time you try this, it is best done in a time and place where you will not be interrupted or disturbed (give yourself at least a half an hour). You might like to have paper and something to write with to record insights and impressions after the process is over.

Find a comfortable position. This is best done seated, but lying down can also work if you're confident that you won't just fall asleep.

Take a breath and feel your body settling in.

Take another breath, letting go of any tension you may be carrying.

Take a third breath and follow it down inside you, focusing your attention around your solar plexus.

As you get relaxed and comfortable, invite your inner child to reveal herself to you.

Where is she?

What is she wearing?

What is her mood, her feeling, her expression?

Does she acknowledge you?

See if you can say hello to her.

How does she respond?

Does she come to you? Maybe she turns her back or looks away, maybe she's angry at you. Just notice what her response is.

In the most gentle and appropriate way you can, let her know that you're here and that you'd like to connect with her and talk with her.

Find out what she needs to feel safe, what you can do for her.

Begin to have a conversation with her. What does she want you to know? What does she need to hear? Chances are she's a little upset with you for not being there for her when she needed you. Maybe she just wants you to play with her, that's totally fine too.

Just truly listen and see if you can connect with her and what she is needing.

See if you can help nurture and comfort her and help her feel secure.

She might be hesitant at first, but stick with her.

If you need to, let her know that you are sorry that you haven't been there for her so much in the past, but that you want to create a different kind of relationship with her, you really want to support her and be there for her.

Continue the dialogue and see what she reveals to you. Continue to play the role of a caring, competent and nurturing adult for your inner child.

If this is difficult for you to get into, you might also reflect back to your own childhood and times and places that were painful for you. What did that little child need to hear? How does she wish that someone would have responded to her in her experiences of pain or time of need? See if you can imagine saying that to your child self in those experiences, and how you might have felt or responded differently if someone were to have told you those things or responded to you in that way. Even traumatic childhood experiences can be addressed in a similar way. Maybe you wish someone had stood up for you or protected you. You can replay the painful event in your mind and then rewrite it as you wish it would have been. You can replay that experience with the outcome you would have desired.

Continue connecting with this child part of you, hearing what she has to say. When you get a sense that things are complete, or you as the adult must move on to other things, ask her what she needs from you in order to feel secure and know that you are there for her. Maybe there's a sign she can give you (or has been giving you!) to get your attention. Maybe you agree to check in with her at various times throughout the day. Some times that have worked well for my clients are in the morning when they wake up or at night when they go to bed. Brushing their teeth can be another time, or at meal times, something that is part of your regular routine. In addition, acknowledging and supporting her whenever you remember throughout your day can be helpful as well. Make an agreement with her about when you are going to be there for her, or how she can get your attention, then keep it! You are developing trust and helping her know that you will be there for her and take care of her and that she can relax and stop being the one in charge.

As you continue through your life, give at least some attention to your inner child each day. Listen to her and make space for the things that she desires or asks for. If you start to feel scared, overwhelmed, or worried about your life (and have identified that it is truly yours), check in with your inner child. Are those feelings coming from her and not from you as the competent adult? Reassure her that you've got her back, that you are taking care of her, that you aren't going to let anything bad happen to her. Be the parent she needs you to be, be the parent you needed when you were little. You have the power to give that to yourself.

If you can separate out each of these parts of yourself, it will be much easier to get through the challenging moments. Usually the one that's feeling scared or freaking out is your inner child, and if you can comfort and support her through the process, you can keep moving forward in your life with competence and confidence.

Chapter Ten
Reset Your Emotional Compass

"Your feelings are not up for negotiation."

JORGE RUBIO

Undo Your Emotional Confusion

As we grow up we often learn to cut off our awareness of what is actually happening around us and what is truly going on with the people in our lives. Perhaps you were aware of things that your family didn't want you to see, so they denied them or told you that you were wrong. Eventually you believed it. Maybe they told you that your feelings were wrong, that you were overreacting, making a big deal out of nothing, or shouldn't feel the way you felt, and somewhere along the line, you believed that too. You accepted what they told you as the truth even though it didn't feel right or make sense to you. If this was true for you, you may have started to wonder what was wrong with you when your experience of reality didn't seem to match with what people were telling you was true. Maybe you even thought that you were crazy.

Chances are, this has created all sorts of confusion and havoc in your life. What in your life have you not been willing or allowed to acknowledge or see? What did the people around you deny even though, on some level, you knew it to be true? How much have you been trying to reconcile your experience of reality with the people around you? Are you still coming up short? A very typical example of this is when a parent does something hurtful or manipulative to the child but tells the child that it is for her own good. The child is having an emotionally appropriate response to how the parent is treating her, and yet she's being told that it's not what it seems and that her feelings are misplaced. The confusion that this creates is great. In some ways it is easier for a child to experience pain or hurt that they can easily identify as such than to experience those things in the guise of love and care, because it doesn't create the same confusion or cognitive dissonance.

What You Couldn't See in Childhood, You Won't See in Adulthood

You have most likely been taught at some level not to trust your experiences of reality and not to see what is actually happening. As a result, you may have cut off your awareness. One of the ways that this shows up in adulthood is that until you recognize what actually happened in childhood and come to understand how you were really being treated it will be difficult to see where in your present life people are doing the same things. If your parents were unkind or manipulative but completely denied it and you haven't been able to acknowledge this for yourself, you'll be unable to be aware or to see when people are being unkind or manipulative to you in adulthood.

For me, this showed up in my romantic relationships. From my parents I got the message that I didn't know how to receive love. *"We love you, we just don't love you the way you want us to"* was their line, which is an easy way of invalidating my experience and telling me that what I desired, what would contribute to me and make me feel loved, was wrong. I was the problem, and if I could just learn how to receive love better, then my experience would change... at least that's what I internalized. It was never them that needed to change. I see how this played out for me in various other relationships. I was unable to see when the relationship wasn't working or when someone was taking advantage of me or being manipulative or unkind. Instead of clearly seeing their behavior, I just thought it was all me.

Regain Your Seeing

I had to learn to trust myself and I had to learn to see. Looking back at all the years I spent working on myself and my issues, the one thing I wasn't allowed to own, to know, to see, is how angry I was at my parents for not being there for me. This was forbidden territory. It was forbidden in part because every time I brought it up it was met with denial and resistance, but it was also forbidden because the little girl in me still needed her parents, and was not willing to risk losing them by going against their reality. I see many people continue to seek love and approval they never got from their parents well into adulthood (either directly from their parents or other parent substitutes). They have trouble establishing themselves in life in their own right and truly breaking free. This was certainly true for me. In my case this came about in part because, when I was 11, I lost a teacher who had for four years been like a third parent to me. I did not even recognize the impact and trauma of this until I was well into my twenties. On a subconscious level I was not willing to lose my actual parents too. I think that if I'd just been able to express and acknowledge my hurt and pain and be angry and pissed off, to truly rebel and find my own identity as a teenager, life could have been a whole lot easier for me.

But I wasn't willing to risk that loss, so even when I did acknowledge my anger and pain to my parents and it was not received, or was denied or invalidated, I put it away and kept up the belief that there must just be something wrong with me. I often felt crazy. I can see now, through all the self-inquiry and personal development, the one place I was not willing to go was to acknowledge how angry and hurt I actually felt by my childhood experiences and that my childhood was not as truly wonderful as so many people around me told me that it was. Because I couldn't see the truth around this issue and acknowledge my true feelings, I felt very twisted up a lot of the time. It was not just with my family that I felt twisted up but with other friendships and relationships as well. All my energy went to appeasing relationships so that people would not abandon me, which of course worked so un-wonderfully.

Your version of this story probably looks a little different, but was or is there some place in your life where you weren't allowed or able to see what was really going on? Are there feelings or emotions that you were never allowed to experience or feel? How much have you been trying in one way or another to keep that awareness and those feelings at bay? How much do you appease your parents or the other people around you? What if you were willing to have an emotionally appropriate response to what is happening? What if you allowed yourself to be angry (or sad, or even happy)? Whatever the emotion is, when you're finally able to process your authentic emotional responses and feelings, which often got shut off or twisted up in childhood, you can begin to reset your emotional compass. You can untangle yourself from the perpetual confusion, and see clearly what is happening and how you're being impacted by the relationships around you.

The Liberating Power of Anger

Anger scares a lot of people, but I have come to see that one's willingness to embrace and experience their anger can be truly liberating. When I was in the midst of sorting out and coming to terms with my relationship to my parents, I was invited to a Transformational Breathwork session. Breathwork is a method of deep breathing that helps you access and release all sorts of emotional experiences. Over our lifetimes we develop specific breathing patterns, often in order to control our emotions. When you again breathe fully, you access the emotions you've been avoiding with these restricted breathing patterns. In my session, I connected to the anger and rage I felt, not so much at what had happened to me, but that I was not allowed to have an emotionally appropriate response to those experiences. I was not allowed to be angry, I was not allowed to be sad, I was not allowed to be upset with my parents for anything that happened in my childhood.

Most of us are taught that anger is bad, anger is mean, anger is something to be transcended and overcome. What if that's not true? What if anger has a life-giving and life-serving purpose? We get angry for a few different reasons, but for me the most relevant one is in response to someone else invalidating us, our experiences or our being. Anger is about standing up for yourself, having a voice, saying *no*, protecting yourself, and restoring balance and self-respect. It's about clear boundaries and reclaiming the sovereignty over your own space and being. Anger is an emotionally appropriate response to these kinds of situations. It is designed to protect you and keep you safe. When you are not allowed to experience anger or be righteously outraged at situations that feel threatening to you, you lose your strength and your power. It becomes a frozen trauma in your psyche.

As I accessed my anger through breathwork, it was a final *no*. A *no* to being treated with less care, respect, consideration, and value than I know I am here for. I owned the truth of my experience and stopped questioning myself and my sense of sanity or feeling confused about the validity of my experience. It was incredibly clarifying. It helped me to take back a part of me and my dignity that had been lost. It felt like I reclaimed my power and my voice and I wasn't going to accept the invalidation of me anymore. It's not rage and anger I took out on my parents–they could not have received it–but claiming for myself the validity of my experiences and the right to my emotional response was hugely liberating.

Being willing to access and express your buried anger, your righteous fury and indignation, thereby reclaiming your ability to protect or defend yourself, just might be what's required to take your power back, find your voice, and reclaim authority over yourself, your experiences and your life.

After my own personal experience with the liberating power of anger, I had a session with Rachel, a client I'd already been working with for quite some time. We'd made a lot of progress around her relationship with her family. Something still lingered though; Rachel had been sexually abused by her uncle. When the abuse happened her family minimized it, and she was never allowed to have an emotionally appropriate response to what had happened to her. In some way Rachel was still accommodating and taking care of other people's feelings and not having her full voice and power. What could be more violating and invalidating than sexually abused as a child? Rachel needed to access her righteous anger and fury at what had happened to her, to have an emotionally appropriate response and to reclaim the power to stand up for herself in order to feel safe and fully empowered in this world. Again I witnessed how being allowed to have the emotionally appropriate response to her experience that she'd never been permitted to have, was truly empowering and liberating.

Ways That You Give Away Your Power

I repeatedly see clients apologizing or making excuses for others' crappy behavior or treatment of them in the guise of understanding. *"I know he's had a hard life." "I understand why he did what he did." "He didn't mean to hurt me."* Understanding and compassion are great, but so often I see this coming at the expense of the person who is being compassionate or understanding. What often happens with compassion is that we remove ourselves and our own experiences from the equation. We try to understand where someone else is coming from, to have a sense of their perspective and why they would do what they did. Sometimes this can be very liberating and healing. However, I so often see this happen in a way that leads the "compassionate" person to dismiss and downplay their *own* feelings and needs about the situation.

Did you give up on you, your feelings and experiences so that you could be compassionate and understanding? Have you used compassion and understanding to avoid feeling your anger, rage or pain? How many excuses are you making for other people's unkindness and crappy behavior, rather than acknowledging its impact on you and choosing to respect and honor yourself? If it hurt, it hurt, and you have every right to feel the way you do, even while having an understanding of other people. What if you were willing to fully acknowledge and own how things feel to you and impact you, and choose what truly feels good, nurturing, and supportive to you?

Your feelings are not up for negotiation. They are there for a reason. They are giving you lots of valuable information about what you are experiencing. They are not wrong, they cannot be wrong. Your feelings are your lived experience in the moment that you are in. As Byron Katie says, "When you argue with reality you lose, and only 100% of the time."

Like many, I was one to constantly argue with my feelings, to tell myself they were wrong, and that I should not be feeling the way that I was feeling. So much confusion cleared up for me when I allowed myself to feel what I feel and acknowledge how I am being impacted by the world around me. Finally I could see, *"Oh, that doesn't feel that good to me,"* or *"I'm not happy with how this person is treating me, I think I'll choose something that feels better to me."* When I acknowledged my own feelings and attended to my own needs, I stopped needing other people to understand or get my experiences and I stopped needing them to change. I stopped trying to get people to be nicer to me, to treat me better, or to like me. I could just acknowledge how they were actually being and choose whether or not it worked for me. The inclusion of my feelings and recognizing the impacts of others' behavior on me has made me more truly compassionate and understanding, and given me greater space to just let other people be.

Rewrite Your Definition of Love

Given that I'd had a lot of confusion in my relationships, particularly around how other people treat me, I came up with a little saying that was incredibly helpful to me: *"Love is love when it feels like love to me."* Around this time I experienced a great deal of conflict with one particular friend. He would say that he loved me, which at moments I felt, but often the way he engaged with me and treated me didn't feel like love at all. In one instance he told me he loved me and I said to myself, *"Wait a minute, this does not feel like love to me, it actually hurts."* I decided to write my own personal definition of love. I did not want to be confused anymore by what others asserted was love for me (but didn't feel like love to me) with what I knew to feel truly caring and loving. This helped me gain clarity about how I wished to be treated. This doesn't have to just be for love either. It could be for any different quality. *"Respect is respect when it feels like respect to me,"* or, *"I care for myself and I know what being cared for feels like."*

"Everyone says love hurts, but that is not true. Loneliness hurts. Rejection hurts. Losing someone hurts. Envy hurts. Everyone gets these things confused with love, but in reality love is the only thing in this world that covers up all pain and makes someone feel wonderful again. Love is the only thing in this world that does not hurt."

MEŠA SELIMOVIĆ

After creating my own personal definition of love, I wrote it out in tiny print and put it in a locket I wore around my neck to remind me of what love truly is to me. I wrote myself a love letter just to remind myself what it feels like to be seen, valued, and loved. Connecting with that made it so easy just to let go of the experiences and dynamics in my life that did not feel loving to me. All of this was so helpful for me that I facilitated the same process with clients who were feeling confused or struggling with their relationship experiences. I even developed a self-study course around this called *Rewriting Your Love Story* that guides you through uncovering the messages, imprints, and subconscious beliefs you got from early life about love and helps you transform them to create your true love story. (Send me a message if you'd like to learn more about this course.)

Reclaim Your Power, Release Your Inner Roar

Where in your life have you been downplaying how you are being impacted by those around you? Where have you disconnected from yourself or discredited your feelings? What if you could trust your experience, trust your perception of things? Where in your life do you need to *feel* and access your righteous anger at the injustices and violations of your being? What would it take to reclaim your voice and your power and unleash your inner *roar*?

Is there some emotionally appropriate response to your life that you never go to have? For many this is anger, but it could also be other feelings like grief or sadness, or sometimes even happiness or joy. If you know there is some emotion in you that needs to be expressed, some power you need to reclaim for yourself, there are many wonderful and completely non-destructive ways to do this. You can do them on your own, though having someone to support you or help you work with the process can be helpful too. Breathwork was a powerful one for me. This does often require a facilitator, but just getting your breath moving and your heart pumping can help with the releasing. Going out in the woods where no one will hear you (and be concerned) and just yelling and screaming can also be a powerful mechanism for releasing, particularly around anger and rage. You don't necessarily need to scream and yell, but I do think it's incredibly important to get your breath going and the energy moving in your body. It's too easy to continue to control your feelings if you don't. We want to get all that stuck energy and vitality moving again. No matter how much therapy you've been to, mental work you've done, or intellectual understanding you have about what happened to you, there is a physiological component that needs to be engaged. Your body needs a way to release the trauma and frozen energy that is there. When I had my breathwork session where I tapped into my anger and fury, I'd already done a lot of work on the issues with my parents and thought I'd resolved them and understood what was going on. My body still carried all that anger, rage and fury inside and being able to release it and find a voice for it that I'd never been allowed to have was truly liberating and healing.

If you're scared of screaming and yelling (maybe it's triggering or was traumatic for you in your life or just not what you need), try putting on music and moving or dancing like crazy. Make sounds, tones, let your voice be free. What do you need to say that you were never allowed to say? What do you need to feel that you were never allowed to feel? How do you take your power back, how do you step up to your empowered self and release your inner roar? Release, let the energy move through your body, let yourself be free. If there is someone in your life that you trust and feel safe with, you could invite them to support you through the process, to hold space for you as you go through this powerful journey. If you think it will bring up more for you than you will know how to navigate on your own, then do please find a supportive and caring person that can help you through the process and out the other side. This can be someone who you know and trust to guide you or this could be someone who is professionally trained to support you in this kind of process.

Another process you can try for accessing your sense of power that has been helpful for some of my clients is to wrap yourself up (you might need help with this) and then break yourself free. It's symbolic of breaking free from the chains that have bound you. The last time I did this we used toilet paper. You could probably use yarn as well as long as it is something you can break yourself free from. A little bit of effort is valuable, but not so much that you feel stuck entirely. Again, the body engagement is incredibly valuable here. As you do this you could think about the "chains" that bind you from which you are breaking free. What has been keeping you from your truth and your power, and how are you breaking yourself free from that now?

Chapter Eleven
Put the Trust Back in You

"You are the greatest gift you have."

STEPHANIE SHANAHAN

Learn to Trust You Again

In the last chapter we talked a lot about how you've learned to cut off your awareness and not trust your emotional experiences. We explored resetting your emotional compass and taking back your power. In this chapter, I want to take you a bit deeper into what it looks like to trust your awareness and your experiences of life, and how you can use this to guide you. When you allow yourself to have your full awareness and you trust yourself, you are truly in command of your experiences and your life.

Sadly, most of us cut ourselves off from our knowing and our awareness by dismissing it. You get a hunch about something and you say, *"Naw, I must just be making this up, I couldn't know that."* Every time you discount or go looking for proof on something you're aware of, you are discrediting your awareness and saying you don't trust it. (Confirmation, by the way, is different than proof, but I'll get to that more later). Imagine if every time someone told you something, you needed them to prove it in order to believe it. How much more do you think they'd be sharing with you? Maybe they'd just go away. This is the attitude a lot of us have with our intuition or our awareness: *Prove it to me first without a doubt and then I'll be willing to believe it, otherwise it's completely false.* Whatever sense you had about something you essentially just eliminated by having that attitude.

The more you trust you, the more you can trust you. Let's say you have some sort of sense or awareness about something, maybe a little hunch, and you decided to lean into it, to trust it, to go with it. Now let's say that hunch turns out to be right. You just got confirmation for what you were aware of that you never could have received if you had just dismissed it outright. Maybe another time you have a sense or hunch about something and it turns out to be wrong, or different than you thought. The tendency here is to go into judgment about it or think that you aren't all that smart or that you can't trust yourself. There are many layers here that contribute to being "wrong" about something. The attachment you had to something being a certain way or turning out a certain way, as well as thoughts and beliefs you might hold about it may influence your perceptive abilities. However, even if you do follow a hunch and it doesn't turn out how you thought, you just gave yourself a bunch more information that you didn't have before.

When I follow what I think is my awareness or my intuition and it turns out not to be what I thought, I have a whole new layer of understanding about what I'm perceiving and paying attention to, and can start to pull out more and more subtle differences. I might be able to discern, "*Oh, this perception is truly awareness I can trust, and this other thing, which felt slightly different or showed up a little differently, was actually something else.*" Part of the ability to develop your intuition and have trust in it is your willingness to go with what you're perceiving, and also your willingness to find out that you were wrong and develop your skill from that as much as from being right.

The more you trust yourself and act on your hunches or intuitive sense of things, the more you can perceive the details and nuances of your awareness. When you look at a painting from far away it could look like just a blur of random colors, but the closer you get, the more nuance and detail you see. Your awareness is similar, and the more you engage it, use it and develop it, the more you will be able to perceive subtle differences.

Have you ever had the experience of "kicking yourself"? Was there something you knew but you didn't fully register or heed it? Later when things play out a certain way, do you "kick yourself" for not paying attention because you knew what was coming and chose to ignore it? That's a good sign that you've been ignoring and cutting off your awareness. What if you know way more than you've been willing to acknowledge? What if you could just learn to pay attention in the first place, and use that awareness to your advantage instead of having an "*I told you so*" moment with yourself later?

Quit Trying to Convince Yourself

I see so very many clients in such conflict with themselves and their awareness that it's painful to witness. Do you ever find yourself arguing with yourself, trying to convince yourself of something that just doesn't seem right, even though you don't have a specific reason why? If you are doing any convincing of yourself or trying to talk yourself into something and it's creating tension for you, you're probably overriding your knowing and going against yourself in some way. You might want something to be a certain way and try to convince yourself that it's right. Do you actually know deep down inside that it isn't? Are you trying to override that feeling to fit with what you want it to be? What's the likely outcome?

I did this a lot with relationships and have seen more than one girlfriend do the same. I've literally talked myself into being in a relationship with someone, even though my senses told me it wasn't the right choice. I did this in part because I bought the lie that I didn't know how to receive love and that I just had issues that I needed to overcome. When one particular relationship was in the process of breaking up, I was able to look back and to reflect. What I was aware of at the beginning of the relationship was just as true for me in the process of leaving. So many things I thought I just needed to work through and overcome were actually valuable bits information about the relationship and the future of the relationship that I totally dismissed or discredited. Talk about kicking myself, and bemoaning the fact that I didn't pay attention to my senses in the beginning! I made a firm commitment at that point to trust myself and my sense of things and to choose what felt good for me and worked for me without reason or justification. Honoring myself and the truth of my experience felt more important than disappointing somebody else. How many people end up married because they haven't been willing to choose this? I had a client that chose marriage because she didn't want to disappoint the other person or hurt his feelings. I'm pretty sure she's not the only one who has done that. I'm also pretty sure you can accurately guess how that relationship turned out.

Give Up Your Reasons and Your Justifications

Needing reasons or justifications for your experiences or your awareness is one of the biggest reasons you might go against trusting yourself. You might think that if you can't justify something to others or make your case, then you must be wrong. Have you ever had this come up in a relationship? You don't want to be with someone, and yet you can't find a good reason to break up that the other person can't argue with, so you just stay in the relationship. What if you didn't have to explain yourself and your choices to anyone, and could just truly choose what is right for you in any given moment? When you truly know something, do you have to justify it to yourself or anyone else, or do you just know it? How easily can you be talked out of it? Would you be willing to just know what you know without need for justification? Would you be willing to just choose what works for you without having to explain or justify it to anyone else?

What if, "Because I want to," or, "Because I don't want to," are all the justification that you need? Or how about some of these as possible explanations for your choices:

"It's just not the right choice for me."

"It doesn't feel good for me."

"I'm not up for it right now."

"I'm just not interested."

"I just want something different."

"It's just what works for me."

"It's just what's right for me right now."

The truth will always make you feel lighter and a lie will always make you feel heavier, so if something is making you feel heavier or all twisted up and confused but you're claiming it as true, it's probably not. Go for that which gives you the greatest clarity and peace, that is your *yes*! You can always change your mind. Drop below the reasoning, the figuring out, the justifications, and explanations. A part of you beyond all that *knows*. Listen to your sense more than to the story or rationale. What does a *yes* feel like, what does a *no* feel like? When you feel into it, what makes you feel lighter?

What Trusting Your Awareness Looks Like

I used to not trust my sense of things at all. In fact, I didn't know they were senses, I just thought that I was screwed up. So often I would argue with my emotional experiences, with my sense of things, especially when they weren't externally validated.

As I began to understand and accept that I was incredibly empathic, I began to get curious about my experiences and inquire into them. One morning I woke up feeling incredibly sad. I didn't understand where it was coming from. With the help of kinesiology I identified that it was connected to my mom. I could have just discounted it at that, but I decided to investigate it. I gave my mom a call and asked her how she was doing. I explained my experience, and asked her if it had any relevance for her. She said yes, what I was describing was pretty much exactly how she'd been feeling at that time. *Okay, so maybe there is something to this awareness thing, and maybe if I keep exploring it, it can become something I could trust.* Not every time I have an intuitive sense of something am I able to have that kind of confirmation, but trying out my hunches and having them confirmed on multiple occasions has given me greater trust in my awareness and understanding.

I had an experience of this recently. I could sense some disharmony in a job I had working with someone I also thought of as a friend. Even though she wasn't saying anything and we weren't even really interacting, I could feel the tension mounting. I felt her stress and anxiety and so much of what was going on in her world. I could have just thought it was me, but I was practiced enough to trust my awareness and sense of things. I tried not to let it get to me. One morning I woke up feeling her and all of this craziness quite intensely. I knew that something was going on. I didn't like the way it felt for me to be aware of all this, but I at least acknowledged that I was aware of her and her reality and didn't just think it was me. That very afternoon she fired me. I wish I'd asked more questions and inquired into my awareness, because I could have known that was what was about to happen. When I got her email, it suddenly all made sense and I better understood what I'd been experiencing that morning. On some level I did know it, I just didn't take the time to articulate it or acknowledge it to myself that specifically.

The Limitations of Positive Thinking

Have you ever tried to employ positive thinking or use affirmations to change your life, only to feel at least slightly disappointed with the results? Perhaps they helped you feel better, but were you disappointed or surprised when they didn't create the outcomes you desired? The problem that I see with positive thinking and affirmations is that they cut off a huge piece of your awareness. It's like putting on blinders and only seeing what you want to see, and then getting surprised by what you missed. I do believe there is a place for positive thoughts and they are certainly a lot more uplifting than negative ones, but what if you didn't have to cut yourself off from any awareness or information you are getting? What if you just stayed curious and open rather than making a negative or positive conclusion?

Let's say you get a funny feeling about a situation you are in and how it's not going to work out. You want to stay positive though, so you use positive thinking and affirmations and completely ignore what you are perceiving. Then, when the situation falls apart or doesn't work out the way you'd hoped or affirmed, you act surprised. What if you acknowledged to yourself that you had the awareness that there were issues with the situation, rather than just trying to think positively about it? If you could see what's really going on, wouldn't that be a lot more helpful?

Another reason affirmations and positive thinking fall short is that you're trying to convince yourself of something you don't believe. There's a tension created between what you want to believe and what you actually experience. In addition, if you're overlaying positive thinking and affirmations on top of your subconscious behaviors and patterns, they aren't going to work so well. Those subconscious beliefs and patterns are there for a reason, and until we can replace them with something else that will accomplish the same thing, those affirmations are not going to be all that effective. If there's something going on subconsciously that makes you feel unsafe in certain situations, then telling yourself, "I am safe, I am safe, I am safe," is completely ignoring and overriding your subconscious reality. Imagine if you're freaking out about something, or feeling very scared and someone keeps telling you that you're fine and there's nothing to be scared of. Most likely you just feel worse because that person has just invalidated your experience and your feelings. If we don't acknowledge and include the subconscious and what it's trying to do for us, then we're doing the same thing to it.

I love the definition that Access Consciousness provides about what consciousness is: *"Consciousness perceives everything and judges nothing."* In essence, consciousness is total awareness. What if, instead of positive or negative, you were just aware? What if you didn't judge, but instead inquired into that awareness and let it inform and guide you? Is it any more valuable to be aware of a tree than it is to be aware of a stone? Being aware of a place where you feel scared or confused is no less valuable than being aware of where you feel happy. It's all just information. So often we cut this off with "positive thinking" or affirmations. If you are willing to receive this awareness and this information, how much more valuable could that be to your life?

I could have employed positive thinking and affirmations when I became aware of the situation with the friend I was working for. It may have changed how I was feeling, but it would have left me shocked, surprised, and potentially hurt when she fired me. Instead, I at least had an inkling that it was coming based on what I'd been perceiving. I was not at all surprised or shocked when it happened. By trusting my awareness, I literally knew beforehand that the end was in sight, I just didn't quite know when or how it was coming. Because of that I was prepared for it, and other than teaching me about awareness and trusting my sense of things, it had only very minor impacts on my life.

Tools for Developing Intuition and Self-Trust

Trusting yourself and your intuition is not something I can entirely teach, it is something you must *do*. In a sense, this entire book is about learning to trust yourself and your awareness. The more you trust you, the more you can trust you. That said, there are a lot of things you can explore that will help you hone and develop that sense for yourself.

One of my number one tools for developing and honing my intuition is muscle testing. When I first started practicing kinesiology I got slightly annoyed with myself for testing practically every single choice or decision in my life. What to eat, where to go, what to wear. What I was really doing was just taking a moment to check in with myself and listen to my intuition. My TK teacher taught that muscle testing is there to help you hone and develop your inner knowing and that there could come a time when you no longer need that outer confirmation. Through the process of muscle testing I've become much more in tune with the subtle energies of my awareness, and can feel the difference between a yes and a no inside me. Many times, I'll be in a session with a client and will already know which way the muscle test will read before I do the test.

How can you use this in your own life? Begin by inquiring into those things in your life that don't have a lot of significance or attachment around them. Maybe you're choosing between eating at two different restaurants and neither one stands out as the clear preference. You could use your muscle testing and see which one you get. You could also just ask yourself which one feels lighter to you and go with that. Anything that you could think to explore with muscle testing you could try. (If you're looking to predict outcomes in the future, however, you'll probably be disappointed with your results. The kinesiology process works best when it is connected to a choice in the present.)

The easiest place to start to develop your intuitive sense is with things that don't feel incredibly significant. When you have a lot of attachment to something or an idea of how you think it *should* be, it will be much harder to hear your intuitive sense clearly, or get an accurate muscle read. Pay attention to the subtle layers that you're perceiving. Ask questions about them, be willing to follow your hunches, and see where they lead. Remember that awareness is a moment-to-moment process, not something that is fixed in time and space. It's not like a decision. Decisions also cut off your awareness and can get you stuck. When you decide something you often eliminate everything from your life that doesn't fit with the decision you have made and are trying to prove right. Awareness just gives you information in every moment, so if you take a step in a certain direction through following your awareness and something shifts, you can include that awareness and make a different choice. Decisions are often fixed in time where as awareness and choice keep moving, changing and flowing.

Ask questions, play with these tools, see what creates ease or lightness for you, experiment with following your awareness, and see what you can learn or discover as a result. Suspend disbelief and self-doubt for a moment, and see what can be revealed to you when you stay in a place of curiosity and wonderment. Be willing to seem crazy to other people, to not have a reason or a justification. Awareness is super light. It's like a tiny whisper, a little feather touch, a hunch. It is often only after trusting yourself or following your awareness that you will be able to see what it was guiding you toward or that it will make any sense.

Chapter Twelve
Other Weird Stuff You Need to Know

"Please be careful with me, I'm sensitive
and I'd like to stay that way."

JEWEL

There are a few other things that you need to know, because if you don't you might get stuck or think that the tools and processes in this book don't work.

Entities

"Entities" might seem like a weird and scary word, but entities are just energies without physical form. They aren't anything to be particularly scared of, but they are important to know how to work with or they could create some challenge and hardship in your life. This might sound super weird, superstitious or hokey, but let me tell you a story that might help you understand what led me to believe this is important.

I took a trip to North Carolina and I stayed in an old mill building for a couple of nights. The first night there I had a very difficult time sleeping. I had lots of weird thoughts going through my head to the point where I was connecting with some suicidal feelings. It was very confusing because I didn't think I really wanted to die, and I couldn't understand what was going on. Fortunately, I had a healing trade planned with someone in the area, which I went to the next day. As I drove to her house, I was still feeling all sorts of twisted up and crazy, and not understanding exactly why. When I got to her house I lay down on her massage table and she asked me what was going on. I started to describe it and she asked me, *"Are there entities present?"*

I just started bawling. Yes, there were. I acknowledged that I'd been aware of some of the suffering and misery of the workers in that old factory. She helped me clear them from my space and I felt much better–but not all the way better. What ensued was a very challenging week. I felt this extreme sense of isolation and separateness from the rest of humanity, accompanied by other very dark feelings. Even the healer I'd been working with around that time was of no help to me. I posted some questions on a forum about entities to see if I could find any more useful information. This was some of the deep, dark, life-alienating, cut-myself-off-from-everyone-and-everything type of energy I'd experienced at various times throughout my life. I hadn't understood why I felt that way or what I needed to do to change it. It was suicidal level depression that didn't make much sense to me because I didn't actually want to die, but at the same time, I felt those feelings so strongly.

One response I got from that forum was completely enlightening for me and helped me permanently change my experience with these energies. What she shared is that entities often don't know that they are dead. They want desperately for someone to pay attention to them, but because they don't have bodies they can't get anyone's attention and they feel completely isolated and just want to die. This dark energy and extreme sense of isolation with suicidal feelings I was having were exactly the kind of thing she was describing.

As I reflected and looked back on my life and my experiences with depression, I could see and identify several times that I'd been through similar things. Something suddenly clicked for me. These unexplainable depressions and suicidal feelings were often not even mine, but connected to being aware of or taken over by entities and not recognizing it or knowing how to deal with it. I learned how to work with and clear entities from my space, and those dark and suicidal feelings went away. Maybe you're skeptical, but what convinced me that there is validity to this is that after my experience in North Carolina I have never gone back to feeling the same level of depression or suicidal feelings. Every once in a while some dark feeling or energy will show up in my space, but as soon as I acknowledge it as entity energy and do what I need to do to clear it, it completely goes away.

This was a huge missing piece of the puzzle for me in unlocking myself from depression. Whether or not I believe that there are disembodied spirits and ghosts floating around and influencing or haunting me or if this is just some energetic experience I'm having, it doesn't particularly matter to me. I know it could seem very weird and far out and it kind of was for me, but the degree of change it created in my life was something I didn't find from any other work or healing that I'd tried. Whatever it is or was, I'm willing to go with the concept of entities and the related tools that helped shift and change the energy. Since that time, I've come to see how much these energies also play a part in other people's lives. This kind of awareness is not easily accepted in mainstream culture, and it is the kind of thing for which people are often labeled crazy. Yet again, it has been my willingness to acknowledge my perceptions of these energies and realities for which other people might call me crazy, that has helped me finally feel sane.

I know this stuff works for other people too. My friend Emily had these intense experiences where she didn't know what was going on. She'd feel all twisted up, weird and confused, and sometimes just curl up in a ball feeling like she couldn't function or move. I would ask her questions about what she was aware of and if there were entities in her space. Then I'd use the tools I learned to help transform and clear them. It created immediate shifts in her reality and she would come back to a place of feeling sane, present and able to function again. This happened multiple times with Emily and has been relevant for other people I have worked with as well.

It is clear to me that Emily has far great capacities to perceive entities, than I do, but that she hasn't learned to acknowledge it or work with it and it has created a lot of problems in her life. Most of what I know about entities I learned from Access Consciousness. If this is something that feels particularly relevant to you or you wish to explore more, I highly recommend checking out the work of Shannon O'Hara and her *Talk to the Entities* materials. She has taught me a great deal and has incredibly powerful tools, information, and insights based on her own experiences that include perceiving and seeing entities throughout her entire life. If you would like to understand and learn more about how to work with and clear these energies from your space, send me an email and I can provide you with additional resources.

Include Your Body

Something I only briefly touch on in this book is the role our body plays. Your body's well-being can certainly affect your ability to function or to get and stay happy. In discovering the keys to unlocking myself from depression, I discovered that one of the keys was physical. If you experience the particular kind of depression where nothing, not even the things you normally enjoy, affects your happiness, there's a good chance your body needs some nutritional support that you're not getting. The way I discovered this was an issue for me, and also my solution, was to visit a health kinesiologist. He was able to identify areas where I was deficient and assign the necessary support and supplements to get my body working well again. It did seem to help, but then I decided that I should be able to fix this with consciousness and self-awareness and I stopped going to see him. It wasn't long after that that I experienced a noticeable dip in how I was feeling and decided to return. I immediately felt better.

For menstruating women, it also might help you to pay attention to your cycle. I know that women hate being told their experience is just PMS, but it could be quite helpful to notice if this is true for you. I would have very dark moods or depressions show up right before I started bleeding, and for the longest time I would get swept up by them and not realize the connection until after it happened. Or I'd get super weepy and emotional and cry a lot. If this is happening for you, then some hormone balancing support might be helpful for you as well. Now, I occasionally have a couple of hours where I get incredibly grouchy and wonder what is going on. Sometimes I do recognize that I'm about to bleed. As soon as I start my flow, the weird, funky, and heavy feelings go away.

If the kinds of feelings I described above reflect your experience at all, I highly recommend looking into some nutritional support for your body.

The tools in this book will go a long way to help you, but if you're still feeling stuck or struggling to have them make a difference, then this may be an important missing key for you.

In addition to nutritional support, there may be other ways that your body needs to be supported and included in the process. If you recall the story I told about breathwork and anger, this was a place where I'd done a lot of mental work but that my body was still carrying the imprints and energy of my history. Your body has its own memory and consciousness, and it may be necessary in your healing journey to find ways to release what is still occurring in your body. There are many wonderful body based processes and supports that can help you. Breathwork, EFT (emotional Freedom Technique) and The Bars along with many other body-based processes from Access Consciousness have been personally helpful. There are also many others. These are processes that cannot be done at a distance or in a book because they require working directly with the body.

Chakras and Chakra Balancing

Chakra balancing once just sounded like some weird woo woo hippie dippy kind of thing and I didn't put much stock in it. Then I had some personal experiences that completely changed my perspective and made me a believer enough that I don't think the information in this book would be complete if I left it out.

If you have never heard of chakras before, here's a very quick overview: They come from ancient Eastern traditions and are considered to be concentrations of energy in your body. There are seven commonly recognized major chakras and many more minor ones. The seven major chakras run from the base of the spine to the crown of the head. Each chakra relates to different energies and qualities within the body. For example, the root chakra at the base of the spine has to do with grounding and survival, and the throat chakra has to do with expression and creativity. There are many other bodies of work written on the chakras which I will not repeat here. If you wish to learn more, you can do your own research and find out more general information including chakra locations, names and colors

What I do wish to talk about is the connection between chakra balancing and your experience of well-being. I didn't believe in chakra balancing until I started having some very intense experiences where I could literally feel the energy in my heart chakra. This energy was often out of balance, and when I was able to balance it, I felt ever so much better.

As I've developed my awareness and my work, my hands have become more sensitive to energy, and I can feel the energy in people's bodies. Often I will give someone a hug and my hand will go on their back at about their heart chakra. I can feel the energy, and often know that if I muscle tested, the heart chakra would muscle test weak. With friends I'm close to, I have done this and given them mini chakra balances that they say have incredibly helped.

I began to explore and play around with balancing my own chakras, and I started to notice the correlation between how I was feeling and how many of my chakras were out of balance. One day I was running errands in town and found myself in this horrible-feeling state that I just could not seem to shake. None of the other tools I had for shifting things seemed to be working. I then tested my chakras and identified that three of them tested weak. I did some work to balance them, and I quickly felt much better. Sometimes, I cannot figure out why I'm feeling so horrible and I'll muscle test my chakras and discover that three or more of them are testing weak. When I balance them it makes a huge difference in how I'm feeling. If nothing else seems to be working for you, I recommend giving your chakras a check.

You can do this by holding your hand over each of them and perceiving the energy. If you don't trust yourself to perceive that yet, or if you aren't that sensitive to your energy, just use the basic muscle test. Hold one hand over your chakra and then connect with your body and see which way it is pulled. If it moves back, there's a weakness, and if it goes forward your chakra is strong. Even if you can't identify whether or not your chakras are off, you can still use the below tools on each chakra and, if it makes you feel better, there's a good chance you just adjusted and balanced your chakras.

The easiest method I've found for chakra balancing is to put the backs of your fingers together and point your fingertips inward toward whatever chakra you want to balance. This completes a circuit and gets the energy moving and flowing in that chakra again. Even just pointing the finger tips of one hand toward a chakra will also work.

Another very simple method for chakra balancing is to visualize filling each chakra up with its corresponding color. Red for root, orange for sacral, yellow for solar plexus, green for heart, blue for the throat, indigo for third eye, and violet for crown. It can be as easy as that. Just focus your attention on each chakra and their corresponding color. Nothing fancy, nothing hard. You can also incorporate sound if that feels good for you. You could point your fingers to a particular chakra and also make a sound or a tone.

Essential oils are a favorite tool for me that seem to create energetic and chakra shift when nothing else does. Sometimes just holding a bottle of oil up to your chakra or smelling it can be helpful. Many oils you can also apply directly to the skin, which can make a big difference as well. Be sure that if you do use essential oils, you are using a pure, high quality brand with a high energetic frequency. Many essential oils are not actually pure, even if labeled as such and can contain other ingredients including synthetic chemicals that can have an adverse affect on your energy not to mention your body and your health. I use Young Living essential oils because I believe they are of the highest quality, and they have made the greatest difference for me (you can order at www.youngliving.com with member number 1442882).

Projections

Projections are one of the things that used to confuse me and trip me up the most. Projections are the stuff that other people put on you about who you are and how you show up in the world that isn't true to you. It's not always conscious on their part, and you are not always aware of it yourself. After I've had an experience that involves a lot of another person's projections, I'm often going *"That was very weird, what just happened"*? It can feel so incredibly strange and twisted up and ever so confusing. As an empath it can be especially easy to get twisted up in other people's projections because it is so easy for you to fit yourself into other people's realities.

Projections are the lenses through which people see you, or think they are seeing you and can be quite certain it *is* you. Often but not always, the person projecting projects onto the other person qualities, personalities, or traits that are present in them that they do not want to see in themselves. If ever someone is being particularly critical or judgmental of you, there is a very good chance that somewhere within themselves they are exactly like what they criticize in you. There is a bit of truth to the saying, *"When you point a finger at someone else, there are three fingers pointing back at you."*

When somebody is projecting onto you, you might think, *"Whatever in the world is going on here, this doesn't make any sense, it's so confusing."* Often what happens is that when people are projecting onto us we try to counter their projections, but because they aren't seeing us or the situation clearly in the first place, it doesn't really work. It's like you're trying to shift their perspective and get them to see you in a different way, but they are wearing funky distortion glasses. No matter what you do or change to try to shift their perception of you or the situation, it won't work very well because they will still just see distortions.

They may also try to convince you that what they are telling you about you is true. I once had a "friend" telling me all the places where she thought I was missing the mark or sabotaging myself. Some of it didn't feel at all true to me. The dynamic that got set up was that either I agreed with what she thought my problems and shortcomings were, or I was just self-deceptive and didn't see myself clearly. Because it was a one-on-one dynamic, it became very confusing. I started to wonder what was real or true and if maybe I was just deluded in my sense of self. Fortunately, she took to criticizing me in the public forum of Facebook where other people saw it. They told her to back off and leave me alone. It was so refreshing to have others validate what my experiences told me was true. This dynamic of projections can become particularly pronounced in the one-on-one relationship and can be an aspect of emotional and psychological abuse.

I had an experience like this with my friend Robin. He was seeing me in a particular way and judging me for being a certain kind of person.

I tried so hard to show him that I was something different, that I wasn't what he saw me as, and yet no matter how I showed up, it didn't change his perception. Finally, I realized that I had no power over his perceptions, and that no matter what I said or did he was going to continue to see things through the lens he believed was true. This was incredibly liberating for me because then I could stop trying to prove to him that I was different than what he saw and just be me.

You can use all the tools in the rest of the book to help you out in these kinds of situations. If things start to feel quite strange and confusing with someone else or you get out of an interaction and think, *"What on earth just happened,"* then there's a good chance there was some projection going on. Ask questions and release any energy that may not be yours. Know that the person you just interacted with was wearing projection glasses and that what you did or said wasn't the problem. What if you were actually fine, and they had some weird energy going on with them that they were telling you was you? Don't try to change it for them because they are convinced that what they see is real, and for them in that moment, since they don't know they are wearing distortion glasses, it totally is. If you can just let them have their reality and not fight them for it, they will either eventually shift their perspective on their own, or you just get to continue with being you and staying connected to the truth of you.

Chapter Thirteen
Challenges On This Path

"Believe in yourself and all that you are.
Know that there is something inside you
greater than any obstacle."

CHRISTIAN LARSON

You now have at your disposal a significant amount of understanding about your experiences and what is truly behind them as well as access to the knowledge, resources, and tools that can change them. When you hit a challenge, or things don't instantly change and improve for you, it can be tempting to give up on them and go looking for some other answer, solution, or program that will help you solve your problem without doing the work that is required. I'm not saying you will do this, but I'm saying that it can be very tempting to blame the process, yourself or the tools when you're frustrated or haven't resolved an issue in the split-second time you think it should take.

There are moments when I still do this. I will think, *"Well, this time there must be something wrong with me; this time the tools won't work; this time I'm truly broken,"* or some version of that. Yet, every single time I do the work and get to the bottom of what is going on for me, my whole reality and experience of life changes. Every single time. When you're in it though, when you're mixed up with other people and their realities, it's so easy to fall into thinking there is something wrong with you. It can feel intense and you may start to believe that it is actually you. You'll forget that you're not crazy, but that you're just super aware of what is happening around you.

I know enough now and have had enough experiences to understand that the *"what on earth is going on, I feel crazy and insane"* feeling is not me. So many times I come out the other side and realize that yes indeed, none of that was me or mine. I was just very aware, and now that I've moved through it I feel sane and back to being myself again. Don't fall for it. Use the tools, acknowledge what you're aware of, acknowledge that this is not you, and be willing to perceive what you're aware of, even if it seems ridiculous or insane to other people. What's true for you will make you feel lighter and restore your sense of sanity.

Awareness Can Be Intense

Awareness can be intense too. Sometimes when we start to pay attention to what we're aware of it can feel more intense, more crazy. As you work with these processes and these tools, your awareness will begin to increase. It may feel like things are getting worse or more intense, but that's just because you're now aware of so much more than you ever were before. You have access to so much more information which will ultimately help you, but at times can feel completely overwhelming. If it feels intense or overwhelming, expand yourself out, make yourself bigger like we talked about in Chapter Seven. Use the tools to create more ease and space.

Sometimes You May Need to Ask for Help

Another challenge you may encounter is that at times you'll be so mixed up, so triggered, or so deep in what is going on for you that it can be hard to get yourself out. There is nothing wrong with that. Sometimes you'll need outside assistance to work it out and come back to a better place in yourself. You can't always see yourself from the inside out, and you might need someone as a mirror to help you from the outside in. I have people that I call that I know will help me sort things out when I've gotten to this place. Choose these people wisely, because not everyone will be able to assist you in a way that works for you. Some "assistance" may just leave you feeling more twisted up, lost or confused. I have had "healing sessions" I've had to recover from because they just twisted me up more and were not at all healing. Clearly, I recommend working with me or someone like me who employs similar tools and processes. If you don't have someone in your life that is able to help you, let's have a chat and see if we might be the right fit to work together.

Do the Work as Soon as You Know You Need It

More than a few times I have gotten to a place that I can't seem to work out or resolve myself. I know there's something I need to identify or look at, but haven't been able to get it on my own. Because I'm a bit stubborn, I often wait and suffer with it, sometimes for weeks before I reach out for help. Every time I finally do reach out, I'm totally impressed with the change it creates and I wonder why I put it off so long. You may be tempted to wait until things are extremely bad to reach out for help. However, if you don't deal with the original issue right away, then all sorts of secondary issues arise.

Imagine something upsetting happens for you and you emotionally withdraw. You continue to go about your life, but something inside you is contracted and off. You engage with others from that place. Your friend wonders why you don't like her anymore and your work and engagement with life suffers as a result. When you finally get to taking care of the original issue, everything shifts and you are back to your true self. However, now, instead of just dealing with the original issue, you're also dealing with the fallout that issue has created in your friendships and your work.

The sooner you recognize that something is off and take the time to address it, the easier it will be on you and your life. It's like course correction: If you turn around as soon as you recognize that you've gotten off course, you'll continue to move in the direction you desire to go without any significant negative impact. However, if you get off course and continue traveling in that direction for any significant amount of time, there's a lot more you'll have to do to get yourself back on course. I am constantly checking in with myself, monitoring what is going on with me and my energy. Any time I'm aware that something is upsetting or taking me out of being myself in the present moment, or presenting a challenge to my forward movement, I do the work to shift it.

If you find yourself feeling stuck or not able to work something out on your own, then you probably just need some extra help and support to get to the root of what is going on for you. Transformational Kinesiology is truly my greatest tool for this and I have never found anything else quite like it. I have tried very many healing modalities and processes, and while each of them offers unique value, I find myself always coming back to TK, or bringing TK to the other work because of the direct access and precision it offers. TK can point you right to what you most need to look at to create the kind of change you are seeking in your life. I interviewed several clients to get their perspective on this work, and over and over again I heard how much they love that the TK process gets right to the heart of what needs to be addressed and can create insights and shifts in a fraction of the time it takes through other methods.

This isn't just tooting my own horn, this is true gratitude and appreciation. I just facilitate the process, and while I do have some experience and intuitive insights that help with its effectiveness, it is truly the process I am working through that makes it so powerful. If you've experienced some shifts and openings through reading this book but know that there is more that you can't access on your own, I highly encourage you to be in touch. The process can hone in right on the places that are most keeping you stuck, and help shift and transform them with ease. I'd love to share the magic and transformative power of this amazing process with you.

Conclusion

"There is a voice inside of you
That whispers all day long,
"I feel this is right for me,
I know that this is wrong."
No teacher, preacher, parent, friend
Or wise man can decide
What's right for you just listen to
The voice that speaks inside."

SHEL SILVERSTEIN

M y hope is that, through reading this book, you have learned to know and better listen to the voice that speaks inside. No one, no matter how wise, intelligent, or psychic knows better than you what is true for you–including me. You, dear reader, are the greatest authority on you. Please don't give that up for anyone or anything. Folks who know you might be able to share their insight, wisdom, or guidance with you, but when it comes down to it, you are the one that has to live with you, and only you can ultimately know what is in integrity with your own being. Of course we all get lost at times, or don't always see ourselves clearly, and input and feedback can be helpful, but please don't let anyone else determine what is true for

143

you. My job as a healer and practitioner is not to give you my answers, but to help you see and perceive your own truth and knowing. I help you see where you are getting stuck and how to free yourself again. I ask questions, we explore together, and if I'm headed in a direction that isn't resonating or feeling true for you, then we find the direction that does and continue our discovery there. I let the kinesiology process guide me.

This is the premise of the whole book–discovering and knowing what is true for you. We began by looking at the context in which you live and experience life, and acknowledging and owning the impacts those contexts might be having on you. Contexts and conditions do matter. Sometimes changing the contexts or conditions of your life can be the most powerful thing you can do to facilitate positive change and greater happiness. Switching jobs, moving to a new place, upgrading the quality of your relationships–when you recognize what you've been tolerating that hasn't been a contribution to you and choose something different, it can make a huge difference in your life. What if you kept choosing the things that make your life better, easier, and more fulfilling, and let go of or move away from the things that don't?

We explored how you're not actually broken and screwed up, but that you work exceptionally well. In fact, when you learn to interpret your experiences in a different way, they can give you lots of valuable information about yourself and your life. When you connect with what your feelings are telling you or get to the heart of what is going on for you, your whole experience can change. Everything has information for you if you are willing to listen. What if your emotional experiences are part of your design for a reason and serve an important purpose and function? What if they are part of your internal guidance system?

The information from this system isn't just about you, it's about other people and situations too. When you can differentiate between what is your awareness of you and what is your awareness of other people, your whole life and your whole experience of life can change. You'll know things about life, about people, about your experiences that you didn't think you could know, and you may be able to connect with, relate to, and contribute to people in a very different way. Sometimes though, being aware of other people and their energy can be very confusing. It can be easy to get tangled up and lose track of what is you and what is them. It can feel intense and overwhelming, and more like a burden than something you'd appreciate. We explored many ways that you can stay connected to yourself and your own energy so that you aren't overwhelmed and tangled up. When you know how to work with it, this level of awareness can shift from being an overwhelming and challenging experience to one that gives you lots of useful information.

Sometimes the information we need, is not readily available and we have to look below the surface to discover what it is. We explored how traditional therapy and many other approaches miss recognizing that what you're experiencing might just be empathic awareness. We learned that so much of what is contributing to how you experience and respond to life is happening at the subconscious level. When we can get to those subconscious layers, it can create amazing shifts and changes in a fraction of the time it takes in other modes of healing.

Many of your subconscious patterns and beliefs were set in place in childhood. While it is not possible to go back and change what happened, it is very possible to change your response and your relationship to it. So often we are still responding to life situations and experiences from places in our childhood that have not been healed or resolved. When we learn to differentiate in ourselves the little child from the competent adult and allow the adult to take care of the child, our lives can work ever so much more smoothly.

In childhood, we were trained not to trust ourselves and our experiences, and as a result we cut off a lot of our awareness about what was happening around us and how we were impacted by it. When we rediscover our emotionally appropriate responses to these experiences, we have lots more clarity about how people treat us, what does or doesn't work for us. We can use our feelings and emotions to give us valuable information about what's truly going on around us. This is the beginning of you learning to trust you again. We explored some of the ways you might be in conflict or fighting with yourself and how you can build and cultivate trust in yourself and your awareness of what is happening around you. The more you trust you, the more you can trust you, and as you do so you will have access to more and more subtle and nuanced information that can help and guide you through your life.

I also included a few other things that have been so important for me and my well-being that this book would be incomplete if I did not put them in. This includes understanding the impact of entities on your mental and emotional health, supporting your body, knowing how to balance your chakras, and understanding the dynamics of projection. The path isn't always easy or without obstacles or challenges, but if you know what to look for and can recognize them as they happen, then you'll have an easier time continuing to move forward. Sometimes it will be necessary to ask for help, and the sooner you do, the easier it will be.

My wish for you is that you recognize just how amazing, aware, and empathic you truly are, and that it leads you to ever increased fulfillment, joy, and happiness in your life. Happiness is not a destination at which you finally arrive, it is more like a beautiful tree that you must continue to nurture and tend for it to fully thrive. I have given you all my best tools for tending your tree and my hope for you is that you will use them to tend your happiness well and to harvest all the amazing and incredible fruits this well-tended tree can give. May you share those fruits and nourish others, and may the seeds of those fruits plant happiness trees for others.

Some folks can read a book and plant an orchard. Others will need further guidance and instruction. If you're not the read-a-book-and-plant-an-orchard type, do not fear, you will not be left to figure this out on your own. Maybe you think this is all great, but wonder how you apply this to your life or particular situation? Or maybe you still don't feel totally confident in trusting yourself and your knowing and would like some further guidance. Maybe you wonder what tools to use to change a particular situation. Perhaps you want to better understand what's going on for you at the subconscious level, but still aren't confident you can get there on your own.

The experience of feeling like I was figuring it out on my own and could not find the help or support I needed is much of what led me to write this book in the first place. I am here to give you support and guidance on this journey. If you have a question, be in touch. If there's something you didn't quite understand or would like more information or elaboration on, be in touch. If you're growing a beautiful tree of happiness and harvesting its fruits, be in touch too, because your success is also my success, and the seeds I have offered you that you have grown into trees are helping me build an orchard of happiness. They are seeds of happiness multiplied. May you cultivate your own tree of happiness and share its fruits with others.

What You Can Do When You're Feeling Blue:

- Is this even mine?

- Am I myself in the here and now?

- Expand out as big as the universe.

- Pull all of your energy back to you.

- Unhook everyone else's energy from you.

- Fill yourself up with your own energy.

- Rise to the occasion, step up.

- Take some time out just to be with you.

- Are there entities present?

- What am I aware of here?

- What is this experience telling me? What information does it have for me?

- What life-serving purpose does this hold for me?

- How can I see this differently?
- What is this showing me?
- Do I need some time and space to myself and to recover my own energy?
- If I took everyone else out of the equation and chose for me, what would I choose?
- Am I being myself right now?
- Is this my inner child running the show?
- Is this my problem, or someone else's problem I've been taking on as mine?
- What am I aware of that I've been pretending I'm not aware of?
- Am I willing to use the tools I have to change this?
- What questions can I ask right now that would give me more insight or awareness?
- What creates more ease and space in my being?
- What feels light to me right now?
- Love is love when it feels like love to me.
- The more I trust me, the more I can trust me.
- What do I know to be true?
- Do my chakras need balancing?
- Is this a projection?
- The truth is always light.

Suggested Further Reading

Anything by Alice Miller, particularly *For Your Own Good* and *Thou Shalt Not Be Aware*

Nonviolent Communication, by Marshall Rosenberg

The Boy Who Was Raised as a Dog, by Bruce Perry

Being You, Changing The World, by Dr. Dain Heer

Love, Medicine and Miracles, by Bernie Siegel

Why People Don't Heal and How They Can and *Anatomy of the Spirit*, by Caroline Myss

Power Vs. Force, by David Hawkins

Joyful Evolution, by Gordon Davidson

You Can Heal Your Life, by Louise Hay

Talk to the Entities, by Shannon O'Hara and www.talktotheentities.com

The work of Gabor Mate

Acknowledgements

So many deserve acknowledgment and thanks, not just in writing this book, but in the decades of soul searching, personal self-inquiry, quest for healing, and work with clients that have served to develop this content. Among the most impactful in the process has been my work with Transformational Kinesiology and everything I have learned and gained from the work and teachings of Access Consciousness.

The people that have made the greatest contributions to me through Transformational Kinesiology include: Deb Wilson, for showing me the power of TK to transform my experiences and my life; Carol Hetrick, my original TK teacher who brought such a depth of insight and facility to the work; and my mother, for all the times she's helped to facilitate some place I'm feeling stuck and can't seem to transform on my own. Even just her listening to me facilitate myself has often made a significant difference.

Deep gratitude also goes to my many clients over the years. I'm deeply grateful for all you have taught me about the inner workings of people and the journey to recovering our true essences. While there are far too many to name, I wish to especially mention Erica, who has been a great fan and encouraging client helping to share and promote my work. Melissa was my first-ever consistent client, giving me the confidence and courage and also the evidence to know that it is indeed worthwhile to carry on with this work. Jenny, Jess, Elena, Heather(s), Lee(s), Monique, Dina, Dani, Lisa, Shen, Tara, Margaret, David, Mark(s), AnnMarie, and so many others—thank you for sharing your journey with me and offering valuable contributions to this work. There are truly too many others to name, and each has provided unique insights, perspectives, and understandings. Some of you may find your stories, in one form or another, articulated in this book.

When it comes to Access Consciousness, I have deep gratitude to Krissy Fitzgerald, as we supported each other in working through and transforming our personal places of craziness. I'm so grateful to have a friend I can call when I feel like maybe I'm totally nuts, a friend who won't judge me because I know she's been to those crazy places too and is just here to help me come out the other side. Krissy has been awesome at helping me through some stuck places or freakouts, even in the process of writing this book.

Beyond that are the countless contributions I've received from various teachers and practitioners along the way, all opening my life up to new insights and new learning. I'm also grateful for the young teenage girl, I think her name is Lydia, who told me she was into weird stuff, like Access Consciousness (really? Me too!), and gave me the *Being You Changing the World* book to read. It helped me keep my sanity through an intense week, and brought me back to the powerful work of Access Consciousness when I really needed it.

I wish also to thank Nicole Finch, who planted the seed that led me to writing this book. Nicole and I met only briefly in this physical reality, but she has been a support and inspiration to me on this journey.

Gratitude also goes to Angela Lauria and the Author Incubator for providing such an easy process and framework through which to speedily translate my ideas and learning into this very book. Many people spend years writing a book. I joke that It took me nine years and nine weeks to write. Nine years developing the content and ideas, nine weeks to actually write it!

To the Morgan James Publishing team: Special thanks to David Hancock, CEO & Founder for believing in me and my message. To my Author Relations Manager, Gayle West, thanks for making the process seamless and easy. Many more thanks to everyone else, but especially Jim Howard, Bethany Marshall, and Nickcole Watkins.

Huge thanks also to the hundreds, if not thousands, of children I have worked with throughout my life. Most of you passed through my life only briefly, but many of you made a lasting and significant impact. Most of you will not remember me, but I still remember so very many of you even by name. You will forever be etched in my memory as the little children you once were. It is through you that I have learned so much about human nature, authenticity, and love, and in many ways, you are my true inspiration and the reason why I do this work. May we all return to the place of pure authentic expression and embodiment of our true essence we knew so well as children.

Thank You

Thank you for being here!

I wish for you to get the most out of this book and the most out of your journey to finding your true place of happiness and well-being.

If you are interested in knowing more, going deeper on your journey or getting some assistance in finding *your* true happy head over to my website www.divineessencecoaching.com and you can schedule a breakthrough session with me.

I also have a special gift for you:

A personal guide

Getting The Most Out of Working with a Therapist, Personal Coach, or Healer

Just visit www.guide.yourhappyguide.com

About the Author

Elana is an author, coach, and healer helping to transform the way people approach mental health and emotional healing. For decades, Elana struggled with her own mental health and emotional well-being, including sometimes suicidal level depression. Trying to identify what her problem was and why she couldn't just be happy, she tried many different things including many spiritual teachings and practices, new-age self-help, therapy, positive thinking, and many other alternative healing modalities.

Through all of this, she couldn't find satisfactory answers, and still didn't feel all that happy. This lead her on her own soul-searching journey, and eventually to unique insights, perspectives, and tools that ultimately freed her from a lifetime shadowed by unhappiness and depression. She uses what she discovered, as well as her natural intuitive and empathic abilities, to help others transform their experiences of mental and emotional turmoil to create greater happiness and a true sense of well-being in their lives.

Originally from New England, she now lives in her adopted home of Moab, Utah, where she was called to move after a visit there in the summer of 2016. When she's not busy working with clients, writing, or growing her business, you can find her out exploring one of Utah's many natural wonders.

Website: www.divineessencecoaching.com

Email: Elana@divineessencecoaching.com

Facebook: www.facebook.com/empathicgifts

Morgan James
Speakers Group

↗ www.TheMorganJamesSpeakersGroup.com

We connect Morgan James published authors with live and online events and audiences who will benefit from their expertise.

Morgan James makes all of our titles available
through the Library for All Charity Organization.

www.LibraryForAll.org

CPSIA information can be obtained
at www.ICGtesting.com
Printed in the USA
JSHW042216310321
13150JS00001B/53